A Surgeon of Hussars

A Surgeon of Hussars

The Recollections of a Surgeon with the 15th
Hussars at Quatre Bras and Waterloo, 1815

ILLUSTRATED

Eighty Years Ago, or the Recollections of
an Old Army Doctor

William Gibney

With a Short Account of the Historical record of the
Fifteenth, or the King's Regiment of Light
Dragoons, Hussars

by Richard Cannon

LEONAUR

A Surgeon of Hussars
The Recollections of a Surgeon with the 15th Hussars at Quatre Bras and Waterloo, 1815
Eighty Years Ago, or the Recollections of an Old Army Doctor
by William Gibney
With a Short Account of the Historical record of the Fifteenth, or the King's
Regiment of Light Dragoons, Hussars
by Richard Cannon

ILLUSTRATED

FIRST EDITION IN THIS FORM

First published under the titles
Eighty Years Ago, or the Recollections of an Old Army Doctor
and
An Extract from *Historical record of the Fifteenth, or the King's Regiment of Light Dragoons, Hussars*

Leonaur is an imprint of Oakpast Ltd
Copyright in this form © 2023 Oakpast Ltd

ISBN: 978-1-916535-68-8 (hardcover)
ISBN: 978-1-916535-69-5 (softcover)

http://www.leonaur.com

Publisher's Notes

Contents

CHAPTER 1

Short Introduction

Whether an introduction is necessary to this small volume I know not, as it is written for my own amusement, and more particularly for the perusal of my children and intimate friends; but some may want to be informed as to who the author was, from whom descended, and what authority he has for all his statements. To be brief, the family name of Gibney, though frequently met with in Ireland, particularly in the county of Meath, is rare in England; originally it was Fitz-Gibbon, and borne by the Clare family, who were among the earliest settlers or invaders of Ireland. But the descendants in process of time becoming more Irish than the Irish, and only too often defying the authority of the Kings and Queens of England, converted it into Gibney; that is, the son of Gibb, having the same signification as Gibson or Fitz-Gibbon.

So far back as the year 1600 we were possessors of property at Clongill, in the county of Meath; my great-great-grandfather marrying, in 1690, Margaret Wesley or Wellesley, a sister of Gerard Wesley, afterwards Lord Mornington. From these, in direct descent, I am, being the eldest son of Michael Gibney of Dormston Castle, County Meath, who died early in the present century. Let this suffice; and now for something which I hope may prove more interesting to my readers.

There is nothing in this world of greater importance to the majority of youths than the selection of a future profession, and yet how often is this selection left to themselves, and that at an age when few are capable of making a choice, or at all events of appreciating what may be most conducive to future interests. Random or caprice has often decided the destinies of most of us, for in our intercourse with the world we see many who in any other situation might have been eminent, but, probably owing to an ill-conceived choice at first, have passed through a long life of misfortune, cursing their fate at having

7

chosen a profession for which they find out too late that they have no taste; and this being so, we may be pretty sure it will never be followed with energy, nor appreciated as much as under other circumstances it would deserve.

Although there may be money sufficient to permit a life of ease or idleness, yet as a rule in youth there is often a strong predilection to follow the profession of their fathers, and at the present day we find many in the law and the Church who are treading in the footsteps of their ancestors, no profession showing this more than physic, where the healing art has been cultivated for generations by members of the same family, and, as may be supposed, with various results as to success or failure.

Although this paternal bias is not my case, as I have shown in the introduction to this book, yet from my early life I had a strong desire to enter the medical profession. My father died when I was but a youth, and at his death Dormston Castle was sold, and I, with several more in the family, left to the care of a most excellent and pious mother, who instilled into me good, sound, and religious principles. In this she was assisted by my paternal uncle, who was then a physician of some note practising at Brighton. He was my guardian, and had the general superintendence of my education, and being a man of strong mind and literary habits, together with my mother resolved that that education should be thorough and liberal. With this intention I was sent to a most excellent school at an expense which my mother, with her now limited means, could ill afford.

However, as I was in all probability to have no other fortune but my talents and industry, the expense was incurred, and ever since I have felt most grateful to my guardian for having thus, as it were, laid the foundation of my future independence—if a man even now, without any fortune, can lay claim to that character. At all events, this education has enabled me to live in that circle most congenial to my wishes, and I can say it without assuming too much, that at a very early period of my life I appreciated good society and associating with literary men. Indeed, I always considered a good education a great advantage generally, and a better introduction to life than wealth with a small stock of mental endowments. However, be this as it may, I had my ideas put to the test most unexpectedly.

An offer was made to me of entering at once into a large mercantile house; by accepting, I should escape further school drudgery and probably become wealthy. But without a moment's hesitation I declined the tempting proposal, and continued at school some time longer, devoting more time than hitherto to study, and acquiring a fair acquaintance with Latin, Greek, French, Euclid, and Algebra; in fact, in all those things which at that time were considered as comprised in the term, "a liberal education."

I may remark *en passant* that we had no short cuts to learning; not everything made easy by abridgments, translations, and epitomes. Cramming was hardly known and little practised. We were expected to have more than a mere smattering of what we were taught; we could not pick out the plums and leave the rest of the pudding. In fact, nothing but painstaking industry and perseverance enabled you thoroughly to acquire knowledge, and to become eligible for an entrance into any of the leading professions. We had certainly the "*Gradus ad Parnassum*," but no other ready road to learning excepting our own exertions. I was naturally studious, and had made sufficient progress in my studies; at any rate I presume this was the case, for my guardian to require my giving him a decided answer as to my choice of a profession. I was spending the Midsummer vacation with him at Brighton, and, after informing me that it was time I left school, desired me to select a profession.

I had accompanied him frequently on his visits to patients, more particularly to those in the country round, and observed how much he was respected and appreciated for his abilities, urbanity, and skill; and having always a hankering after physic, as I have observed elsewhere, I at once informed him that it was my fixed resolve to follow his profession and qualify at one of the universities. He said:

> Think a little more upon it, my dear fellow. It is a most precarious business, full of difficulties and disappointments, requiring tact, skill, health, perseverance, and untiring industry: besides, you have no fortune, and I fear for these many years to come your wants will arrive faster than your fees, and that you will never get a crust until you have no teeth to chew it. Think well over it for a few days, and then tell me your mind.

The few days had already transpired when I told my respected uncle that I had well considered the matter, and was determined to encounter the difficulties, so still clung to the medical profession. My resolution seemed not to surprise him, and from his own position towards me he thought it natural enough that I might wish to tread in his steps, and from that date he did everything he could to forward my views. Ultimately it ended in my wardrobe being considerably added to, and at the box office of *The Bull and Mouth* in London to my taking a place outside the mail for the city of Edinburgh, where I was to commence my medical studies at the University.

It was a most dreary night at the end of a cold October, snow falling very soon after we had got clear of town, causing me to feel half-frozen. However, on the second night we reached York, where I slept, worn out by the cold and continuous travelling; indeed, I felt assured that if I spent another day and night on the outside of that coach I must fall off through extreme drowsiness and inability to withstand the cold; but a good night's rest had refreshed me, and after seeing the minster I resumed my journey to the North. It was still bitterly cold, but I managed to get through the night, and later on, when we reached Berwick, four gentlemen inside passengers, pitying my youth, asked me to enter inside with them, and accepting their kind offer, for the remainder of the journey I sat alternately on their knees.

One of my fellow-passengers, a Mr. Roxborough, I discovered was a student of the University returned to take his degree. He was excessively talkative, used very grand terms, and doubtless thought himself to be among the clever ones of creation. Afterwards I met him frequently at the various classes and in private society. Eventually he obtained a large practice at Hull. He was very handsome and had a good address, to which qualities some attributed much of his future success.

After a bath, changing my attire, and making a very substantial breakfast, I went forth to deliver my various letters of introduction, among these being one to a recently dubbed Doctor of the preceding summer. He was very kind in instructing me how to proceed during the first year of my college life, and advised me to take up my quarters in the boarding-house in which he was residing. The term "boarding-house" is somewhat beyond its merits. There were but five of us students in it, but we seldom met excepting at meals, and these were presided over by the landlady herself, Mrs. Jobson, a good, homely kind of woman in her way, but not particularly refined, and whose fare was seldom such as to induce dyspepsia so far as variety went; although it was sufficiently ample to serve all the wants of the inner man; as to drinking, we never had anything at Mrs. Jobson's but table-beer, and that not of an exhilarating quality. It was not sparkling ale of the kind for which Edinburgh is famous, though that, not unlike some of the professors, contains more froth than substance.

Under these circumstances our meals were not prolonged, and we could not afford wine to enliven our conversation; but after a few weeks' intercourse we had learned each other's peculiarities and characters, and being in different degrees of progress in our studies, the more advanced did not waste time by imparting their acquisitions upon the juniors, and, the meal ended, each went about his own business. However, it may be expected that I give some account of my companions at Mrs. Jobson's Boarding-house.

First, my recently dubbed friend Pindar deserves a conspicuous place. He was the son of an old practitioner in the city, who having been prosperous in the business, was determined that his son, by the possession of a degree, should take a more exalted position in the profession than he himself enjoyed. Now, whatever else may have been my friend Pindar's qualifications, I fear his personal appearance and the garb he assumed would militate against his future prospects. To an awkward exterior he added an obsolete style of dress, consisting of short black breeches, silk stockings to match, and his hair powdered and terminating in a long *quieu*, necessitating for its correct arrangement a daily visit from the barber. Poor Pindar had the further misfortune to be exceedingly short-sighted, for which he always wore spectacles, or rather goggles, their large size rendering them particularly conspicuous; added to which the wearer had an abominable trick of poking his nose close to your face when addressing you.

In fact, Pindar aped the formality of the old school, imagining, I suppose, that it offered certain advantages; he never answered you at once, but, turning up his chin, and commencing with a "hem" or a "hah," as if collecting his thoughts, took time in communicating his sentiments. He was, however, like his great namesake Peter, a bit of a wit in his way, often saying very droll things, creating a laugh, though not so much at the dryness or wit of the things themselves, as that such remarks proceeded from so exceedingly formal and periwigged a personage. When he himself joined in the laughter he appeared to forget that the barber had pomatumed his hair and *quieu* to the most rigid pitch of doctorial gravity, causing the tail to flap against his back, and the powder to fall off in small showers. Dr. Pindar, moreover, was a great lover of music, and played a little on the violoncello, probably more to his own satisfaction than that of the rest of the inmates of our establishment. When at our studies, being disturbed by Pindar's music was rather a trial.

Poor Pindar soon left us, and tried his success, or rather non-success, in the city, where I met him some years after; but he had received no encouragement. He was, however, happy in his big fiddle, and certainly derived more enjoyment from its harmony than from a superabundance of fees. Eventually he gave up private practice, entered the army, and I next heard of him when I was myself quartered in the north of France. In the innocence of his heart, he wrote to me asking me to send him a horse to the moderate distance of fifty miles, so that he might ride over and see me; of course, compliance was impossible, and soon after we shifted our quarters.

It was not until twenty-five years later that we met, when he entered my study at Cheltenham. Like a wise man, he had stuck to the service, had retired on half-pay, and, being still a bachelor, had the wherewithal to make himself comfortable, and no rival power to entice him from the fascinations of his beloved fiddle. I have ever felt grateful to him for the hints he gave me at the commencement of my university career.

Next to my friend Pindar I shall mention Mr. Longley, who was then completing his second year of collegiate life. He was a man of exceedingly retiring habits, very taciturn in society, and withal devoted to study. In person he was dirty and in dress slovenly, abhorring soap and washing generally. However, he did not trouble us with his company for very long, but took himself off to his little den, inside which none were admitted. He was one of those morose and forbidding kind of people, whom none like and with whom it is impossible to be friendly.

By way of contrast to Mr. Longley, at the opposite side of the house lodged a rollicking, merry fellow called Banfield, who, having secured the promise of a surgeon mate's position in the navy, was, as he supposed, qualifying himself for that situation by leading a somewhat irregular life—larking in the streets, attending all the theatres, and devoting himself far more to the jolly god than to his studies. He was always in difficulties, borrowing money, and, when he could not do that, sold his books to raise the required cash; moreover, he was very mischievous, and shortly after my arrival initiated me into the practical use of phosphorus, by informing me that if I wrote with it on the wall, the impression would be seen for hours after in the dark.

So, one day, when the maidservant was elsewhere, I wrote "Repent" on the wall at the foot of her bed. After the poor creature had put out her light and turned in, we were aroused by loud screaming, and then all was silence. Next morning, poor Mary, who was our maid-of-all-work, including cook and butler, appeared at the breakfast deadly pale, and afterwards informed her mistress that a spirit had visited her last night, and, believing that she had but a short time to live, she intended altering her ways for the future. So sudden a change rather alarmed the mistress, who previously had often caught Mary in various *peccadilloes*, and, taking us into her confidence, concluded that Mary "was awful daft suddenly." However, Banfield and I kept our countenances, and the whole thing remained an enigma to Mrs. Jobson, as Mary could not be persuaded to tell the particulars of her vision. Her fright and good resolutions soon evaporated; and when, later on, she observed me experimenting with phosphorus, I daresay that she made a good guess at the agency whereby the portentous word "Repent" was affixed to the wall in her bedroom.

If our small establishment could boast of a very big fiddle much practised upon by my eccentric friend Pindar, we had also to put up with the scrapings of another lodger on the violin. Unfortunately for us, Mr. Bradshaw was but a beginner, and the trial to our nerves and tempers was great. He was a very gentlemanly young fellow, then studying at the Humanity classes; and, finding Greek and Latin some-what dry food for the mind, he exercised his voice and scraped away at the violin between the intervals of study. He had some taste, and, being a general favourite, an excuse was made for his eternal scraping; but nothing is more abominable than to be made an unwilling listener to a beginner on any musical instrument.

We were going music mad, and so I have no right to complain, as I myself was learning the flute; and when it happened that we three—Bradshaw, Pindar, and self—were in the musical vein, and Banfield in a merry or noisy mood, we were frequently interrupted by a loud howl from Longley, who, popping out from his den in a dirty dressing-gown and dirtier night-cap, would rave, storm, and beg us for "God's sake" to desist, as we were driving him mad.

I met Bradshaw many years afterwards. He served for pension in the navy, became Chairman of Quarter Sessions, married well, and, having a large family, came to Cheltenham for its educational advan-tages. At the end of so many years we were, of course, much altered, and I did not recognise him when he entered my study; but we soon forgot our years, were young again, and spent many agreeable days together. Like myself, he still kept up his music, and now played well. So much for our Edinburgh practisings; and with this ends the history of such composing the society at Mrs. Jobson's boarding-house.

CHAPTER 2

The Professors

I was, of course, soon initiated into the usual routine habits of a medical student at the University of Edinburgh, attending lectures on chemistry, anatomy, *materia medica*, hospital practice, and so forth during the day, and at night either writing notes of these lectures and reading up, or joined Pindar and Bradshaw in a little musical recreation and mutual instruction. Of pleasures I partook in extreme moderation, partly from my purse not allowing me to join in them, and more because I grudged the time taken from my studies, for I saw the necessity of pursuing these with energy. I was very punctual in attending lectures; and, notwithstanding the various degrees of interest each professor gave to his discourse, I did my best to listen, and I suppose swallowed as much as my neighbours.

With Doctor Hope's chemistry I was highly pleased, although, from my youth and inexperience, I am sure that his excellences and elegant experiments were but partially valued and understood. Hope was a great fop in his way; his person was always rigged out to the greatest advantage, the hair neatly powdered and adjusted, and hands and arms put out so as to be observed. He was the neatest experimenter I ever saw. Indeed, so thoroughly did he understand his subject that his experiments seldom failed; he was most methodical in the arrangements of his notebook and the various apparatus to be used. So much was this the case, that did any of his assistants in any way misplace his paraphernalia, he was sure to be in an ill temper during the whole lecture.

He was naturally an irritable man; a little noise or underchat among the students, or the late arrival of a pupil, would fidget him excessively, and then he would threaten that, in case he was again disturbed in his proceedings, he should request the Senatus Academicus to mark their serious disapprobation of such conduct. He was, however, a great

14

favourite with the ladies, to whose little coteries, at that time pretty numerous in Edinburgh, he was a constant guest. In private practice his success was small, but his *éclat* was great; and, being a bachelor, all comforts were amply supplied. He died rich, and though so much appreciated by the sex, yet he never ventured to commit his happiness to any one of them.

As a contrast to Hope was the Professor of Anatomy, Doctor Monro, or, as he was more familiarly termed, "Sandy Monro." To a rather forbidding exterior he added an uncouth gait and rough manner. He was untidy, wore his shoes down at heel and generally untied, trousers ill-fitting, always of a dirty grey colour; waistcoat, cravat, and all in keeping. Then he flopped his hands about as a turtle does its fins; and these hands, from cold or by nature, were red as raw beef. Sandy had the reputation of being so stingy as never to allow himself or his pupils half fire enough in the dissecting-room or at his lectures.

He had an odd habit of suddenly shrugging up his shoulders after the manner of Frenchmen, and was much given to making references to his father and grandfather, who certainly were eminent in the profession; but Sandy was too indolent and mean to tread in their footsteps. Later in life he published some works, which, however, sold badly, and never gained him much reputation.

The medical school did not gain *éclat* by his lectures; he might have been clever, but knew not how to impart knowledge to others. I yet well remember his parading himself round his little arena, where he stood during the delivery of a lecture, and exhibiting the action of the muscles of the ear, proving that in the human subject we may imitate the ways of the minor animals of creation. At the conclusion of his remark, a sub-audible bray came from a distant part of the lecture-room, tending not a little to excite the risible faculties of the class. However unpalatable or unpleasant, nevertheless it was a good and contemporaneous illustration of the professor's lecture. I saw Monro twenty years after this, very little changed. He seemed to be in a fair way rivalling his father and grandfather in longevity, if he did not in anything else.

This season I likewise attended Doctor Barclay's lectures on anatomy and physiology, and in his way the doctor was quite an original character. At first, he was intended for the Church; indeed, I am not sure whether or no he was not actually in it—which accounted for his habit of frequently introducing religious phrases and scriptural quotations; but, on the other hand, these were too often seasoned with jokes, doubtless amazingly relished by many of us, though poor and out of place. Not improbably we carried home more of the jokes than we did of the anatomy.

Barclay was a tedious lecturer. He kept us nearly two months on the bones, and joked on its being a dry subject. He was fond of quoting himself and introducing *his* anatomical nomenclature, eventually becoming terribly prosy and tautologous—so much so, that towards the end of the season pupils were conspicuous by their absence. Barclay, with his jokes and broad Scotch, was a favourite with his countrymen, who insisted upon his being a very clever fellow. There was also another lecturer on anatomy residing in Edinburgh—an extremely gentlemanly man, well up in his work, and with a neat delivery—Doctor Gordon. I attended some of his lectures, to my great advantage.

Had he lived, his prospects were promising, and without doubt he would have been popular and successful. Doctor Gordon's private lectures on anatomy never would have had so many attendants, had the University Chair been properly filled; but Monro's want of tact, or perhaps of talent, caused the beautiful anatomical theatre of the university to be almost deserted. Indeed, in my time he had not one hundred and fifty attending him, and of these many would have kept away, had not the rules of the University required their being present. If I remember rightly, these were all the lectures I regularly attended during my first season, which, with occasional visits to the infirmary, writing out lectures, and close study, occupied nearly all my time.

By the advice of my friend Pindar, I became a member of the Royal Medical Society, which consisted for the most part of young students who had made progress in their studies. Each week a paper or two was read on some medical subject, and afterwards debated upon; and, as may be supposed, not a few had vanity enough to venture opinions, even at times aspiring to the higher regions of speech-making. Of course, among so many young men of different standing in the University, none of whom had yet been engaged in practice, much was not to be expected in the way of facts, but theories and rash opinions were as common as blackberries in autumn. The ancients were quoted, the moderns criticised, and the whole conducted so learnedly and correctly that it formed a very tolerable debating society; and as our lucubrations were recorded in the big book in front of the president, many thought they were already on the first landing of the Temple of Fame.

Bores were numerous, one especially so. He had been originally a dissenting minister, but, cutting divinity for physic, was now pursuing his studies at rather an advanced period of life as compared with other students. He spoke on every subject—being volubility itself—and was quite obtuse in taking the hint that we had had enough; coughing, hemming, and scraping shoes over the floor passed unheeded. He would have his say. Sometimes we were honoured by the presence of the old practitioners in the city, and then we were more cautious.

These could be bores too, if their pet subjects were broached. One of them, rather a constant attendant, had published a book; and whenever *digitalis* happened to be introduced into our discussion he would bore us with long dissertations upon its properties—whether a stimulant or sedative—condemning everyone who disagreed with him, and occupying our time very unprofitably.

Although, as a matter of certainty, there must have been a great deal of trash spoken among so many very young men composing the Medical Society, yet I have no doubt the very meeting of students to discuss medical subjects led to investigation; besides, the desire of speaking before a public body would induce many to read closely, and, so far as possible, obtain a complete knowledge of a subject. They were thus, as it were, led on gradually to the paths of science, and I have seen in after life many of my Medical Society friends become eminent in the profession and most popular lecturers, among whom I need only mention the late Doctor Henry Lee, Marshall Hall, and others.

As a perfect novice during the first season of my sojourn at Edinburgh, of course I never joined in the debates, but gathered up crumbs of knowledge, found great pleasure in attendance, and formed friendships which have adhered through life. At the end of the season the Medical Society wound up its proceedings with a dinner. We met at one of the fashionable hotels, and as I was as well able as any of the members to enter upon this discussion, I did full justice to the viands, spending an agreeable evening—the more so as there were no very long speeches to listen to, I joined but little in private society or in public amusements, I had no time to spare, and my introductions were few.

Beyond an occasional dinner at my banker's, and now and then an invitation to one from an old Irish Peer, Lord F., a friend of my uncle's at Brighton, who was passing the winter at Modern Athens, I seldom went out. Once I can remember feeling very awkward, when invited to dine by the Earl of F., at being forced to appear at his lordship's table in my blue dress coat, and not in sombre black evening dress, when all the world was in mourning for the Princess Amelia. A young coxcomb and a youthful peer eyed me with great contempt; but my kind host was all civility, and made me go with him later on to a concert at the Assembly Rooms, where my unloyal trim probably passed unnoticed.

I cannot omit this opportunity of recording the unvarying kindness of Lord F. He often came up six flats to see me in my lodgings; and now, at this day, I think I see him enter, with his open hand and rubicund face, inviting me to join the family circle. His son and heir was not so attentive. He was a vain and conceited prig, very bigoted in religious opinions, and cared not to be decently civil to those not of the same way of thinking.

Although, as I before said, in those days I did not join much in private society, yet among the students I made many acquaintances, and we frequently had little reunions in the shape of small suppers and occasional midnight rambles in search of adventures. Only once did I get into a scrape at these, and this was in upsetting a watchman. I had a night's lodging in the police station as a penalty, a judicious sprinkling of silver coins enabling me to escape with this short incarceration.

As I did not purpose remaining at the university during the summer months, when the Professors had finished their courses, I made arrangements for proceeding to Dublin, where my mother and the rest of the family now resided. It was a long and somewhat wearisome journey by coach to Dumfries and Stranraer, then across the Channel by packet to Belfast, and by coach again to Dublin, railways and steamboats not being yet invented. Nothing particularly occurred on the way; but I noticed two things: that the West of Scotland was extremely barren, and also that numberless urchins of about ten or eleven years of age took snuff and chewed tobacco. These snuffy-nosed brats crowded round the coach when we changed horses, begging for bawbees. The contrast on crossing the Channel and arriving at Belfast was marvellous. The country hereabouts, more particularly at Hillsborough, was well cultivated, the peasantry evidently well-to-do, and private residences far more numerous than in Scotland.

Travelling all day and nearly the whole night at length brought me to Dublin. A short sleep from daybreak to breakfast time at the hotel, and that meal despatched, I drove off to my dearest mother's house. Home! where I found a right loving and hearty welcome. A new home to me, for I had been absent from all for more than two years. Thousands of questions asked and answered, prospects discussed, domestic matters explained, but as far as love was concerned nothing altered.

CHAPTER 3

Mulchupy castle and its Doings

Having very closely attended to my studies for the past two years, I found myself soon after arrival at Dublin somewhat out of health, and to be sooner reinstated resolved to pay visits to various relations and friends; doubtless believing that among them I might be considered a person of merit, an embryo doctor, with more than a smattering of medical knowledge and terms; but alas! In this stream of life, the current rarely runs smoothly, and as my luck would have it, an old county Meath friend and distant relation whom I had last seen in London, invited me down to his place in the country to spend some time with him, his wife, and daughters, enjoying to the full a variety of field sports; a taste for these having been early acquired under my relative's instructions; so accepting the same with no little pleasure, a short time later saw me on the top of the long coach *en route* for Navan, near which town my host resided.

The queer old conveyance was full of passengers inside and out, and a most motley group they were. Jokes and flashes of wit passed freely among the travellers, more especially among the gentlemen occupying the inside of the coach. Some of them not satisfied with this, played practical jokes on the carmen and peasantry passing along the road. "Pat," says a gentleman to a man quietly walking alongside of his horse and car, giving the animal the benefit of his weight up the hill, "hasn't your horse lost a shoe?"

To which Pat immediately replied, breathless with the exertion in overtaking the coach, leaving his horse and car standing still meanwhile, "Och! long life to your honour for letting me know," and scampering off returned to his horse, commencing a search on the road for the lost shoe as he did so. He might have spared himself the anxiety and trouble, had he been less obsequious, good-natured, and, I regret to add, trusting.

I reached Mr. Tom Tickler's house before dinner, meeting with a most cordial reception from cousins, host, and wife; the family consisting of Tom's two sisters, Anne and Jane, William his brother, and numerous servants. To describe his abode, place, or castle is no easy matter, it being a combination of oddities, by no means unusual among the Irish gentry of that period, who frequently availed themselves of the rooms yet habitable in the many old castles common enough in many parts of the country.

Now, my friend's residence was dignified by the title of Mulchupy Castle, although literally there was barely an entire room or remnant of the old castle occupied by the family, with the exception of the ancient dining-hall, which had been converted into a modern kitchen, and an old guard-room turned into a dairy. Round the ancient precincts of this castle my relative's ancestors had erected various straggling buildings out of the material lying about, and these from time to time, as each generation needed, had been joined together by passages and more rooms, so that at last there was accommodation enough and to spare; but it required some time for a stranger to become acquainted with the geography of the situation.

These various structures, with the gable end of the old castle covered with ivy, formed an irregular square, and across this square some of the family were obliged to seek their bedrooms, and the servants to carry in the dinner from the kitchen to the dining-room; so that on blustering nights and cold winter evenings candles were blown out in one's progress to a bed chamber, the person half frozen to death, and the roast mutton considerably chilled before reaching its destination. Of course, Mr. Tickler was not responsible for these little inconveniences, but one could only wonder why his ancestors had not rebuilt some of the rooms in the old castle in the first instance, which would have cost less and at considerable greater comfort to past, present, or future generations; however, grumbling could not mend matters, and, Irish like, Tickler on coming in for the property found things thus, and was contented to let them continue.

In those days Irish gentry did not look much to elegance, decoration, or even comfort in their mansions. Sporting was the chief consideration. Tickler had married very early in life, coming in for the property after a long minority; and having thereby a fair supply of ready cash, he did as my countrymen did and yet do, circulated it freely and thoughtlessly, started a tandem, kept many carriages, plenty of hunters, and had the house always full of company. This could not last for ever, and at the time of my visit cousin Tom was trying to draw in his horns and pay off the portions due to his younger brothers and sisters by raising mortgages right and left.

Notwithstanding this attempt at economy, the open house system continued, and horses were at the command of all who then formed the society at Mulchupy Castle. I found myself quite at home among them; and as Tickler and his wife seldom went out beyond the confines of the estate, the remainder of us enjoyed ourselves amazingly in riding about the country, shooting, fishing, reading, and indeed in all the recreations usually obtainable in a country house and fine estate. To me, a very young man, naturally studious, and whose life had known little else than the discipline of school or college, the present was all enjoyment and I revelled in it. Miss Tickler, the elder sister, troubled us but little; she was fond of reading and drawing, and being engaged to be married, thought it correct to be sedate, and remain at home.

Her sister Jane was of a very different character, full of life and spirits, and up to every kind of fun and enjoyment, extremely well looking and consequently had many admirers. In her company one was attracted far more by the charms of her conversation, even flow of spirits, naivete, and amiability, than by the fascinations of her person. She was really so agreeable, so attractive, so witty, and withal so perfectly correct in her deportment, that her beauties of person were fairly eclipsed by her other more fascinating qualities.

As we were pretty much of the same age, daily thrown together, moreover cousins and old acquaintances, we were left to pursue our own courses, so it need not be wondered at that, thus exposed to her fascinations, I acknowledged their potency, and in the end saw myself completely vanquished. I was willing to think that my attentions were by no means disagreeable to her, though I was rather youthful, the younger of the two, but old for my age.

In my long life I have seen this incongruity of age, even when the difference is much greater, have various results. In early life it does not so much signify as far as a few years are concerned, but as we jog on towards the end, or perhaps it would be better to say towards the middle, this disparity of years is frequently attended with unhappiness. A great disparity in years ought to be a decided obstacle to marriage, and parents may say and do what they please, but they cannot unite summer and winter, or join two hearts together which have not, if I may use the expression, the same physical susceptibilities.

I had now been several weeks a guest at Mulchupy Castle, and the time for departure had arrived. The idea of separation from my beautiful cousin was a sad sorrow to me, and to avoid this I was willing to throw physic to the dogs and turn agriculturist; to give up all my professional prospects for her sake. It was an instance of extreme folly, and only excusable in love and youth. A letter from my mother desiring my return necessitated parting.

Chapter 4

Enters Trinity College

Certainly, I had trespassed for a long time on the good nature of my country relatives, but leave them I must, and promising to comply with their request that I would renew my visit before again leaving Ireland, I started for home.

Often since I have thought of the great influence exerted over me at this early period of my life by this love affair, and how I was willing and anxious to sacrifice everything to be in my cousin's presence, at any rate not far away from her. Well, I loved as honestly, truly, and unselfishly as a young fellow can and should love.

On my return home, I was met with every token of love and affection from my mother and sisters; though the latter badgered me most unmercifully on my transactions elsewhere, for I could not conceal from them how great an impression had been made upon me by the late visit to our cousins at Mulchupy Castle. My sudden objection to follow the medical profession and desire to take to a country life, farming my own estate, received but little sympathy, nor could I make them see that I might do as well in tilling mother earth as in physicking His Majesty's subjects. I forgot then that capital to a large extent was necessary to success in agriculture.

However, my mother was peremptory, told me she wished me to enter the medical profession, and added as a soother that as a physician I might ask my cousin to become my wife, but not as now circumstanced. I did not take to the collar kindly; reading medical works was as nauseous as black draught, and I infinitely preferred novels and inditing poetry. I don't suppose I was more foolish than others in a like predicament.

My country visit was renewed speedily, and it was the old, old story, and I left happy in the thought that at some future day cousin Jane would become my partner for life. It did me no harm, and instead of returning to Edinburgh I made preparations for attending the winter classes at Trinity College.

In those days the medical session of Trinity College commenced in November, and was opened with pretty much the same formality as at Edinburgh; the Professors appearing in their red robes, which after certain preliminaries were exchanged for the more humble garb of black coat, silk stockings, hair powder, and white neckcloths.

For the present I was advised to confine myself to a repetition of anatomical lectures, clinical lectures, demonstrations on, and dissections of, the dead body. This I did, and I found my time fully occupied, and I trust improved thereby. I became impressed with the value of studying regularly, more extensively, and in systematic order.

Doctor Murtigan, the professor of anatomy, was a great improvement on Dr. Munro and old Mr. Barker, although a most philosophical chemist was by no means so agreeable a lecturer as Doctor Hope. Compared with the numbers attending lectures in Edinburgh University, Trinity College certainly did not shine to advantage. There were but few pupils, and these for the most part put in an appearance from the necessity for their being present at so many lectures, preparatory to receiving a degree in medicine.

In this respect the various classes of the Royal College of Surgeons in Dublin had many more pupils; although perhaps the Professors were not superior in point of talent to those at the university. So many young men were wanted for the army and navy, where of course a thorough knowledge of surgery was absolutely indispensable, that it was not to be wondered at. However, we had some advantages, the anatomical preparations, the demonstrations on the dead body, and the chemical experiments were nearer the pupils, consequently more easily seen, and the lectures themselves better heard.

Old Professor Murtigan was very popular among his pupils. His looks were indicative of good temper, a perpetual smile illuminating his countenance, and his appearance generally was greatly in his favour. He was the very pink of neatness, and to my mind demonstrated and explained his subject admirably. This was the last course of anatomy he ever delivered, and was then occasionally assisted by a Mr. Wilmot, a very good surgeon, but by no means an attractive lecturer.

Doctor Barker, the professor of chemistry, was, as I said before, a very philosophical chemist, but neither fluent in his delivery nor yet always successful in his experiments, hence it became extremely tiresome to listen to him, and towards the end of his course the benches were all but deserted. In private life he was very much respected, but as a lecturer pre-eminently inferior to Professor Hope of Edinburgh,

The room for practical anatomy upstairs was very well attended, and as it was the place where my first attempts at dissections were performed, I own that I did not much like it. The horror of the surroundings, the ghastly look of the dead bodies, mangled and corrupt, legs and arms on one table, trunks and heads on another, bones, often half divided, lying on the floor mixed with various instruments for injecting blood-vessels, and old rusty surgical implements which had served the purpose of operating on dead subjects for many years past. In fact, everything around looked like a charnel-house, so that I, quite a young man and a novice, was disconcerted, not to say horrified, at the scene before me.

However, I suppose custom like poverty makes one acquainted with strange associates, and stranger scenes into the bargain. The older hands exhibited none of this squeamishness. On the contrary, I doubt if there was another place in Dublin where more jokes were cracked, more wit perpetrated, or more fun carried on than in this very dissecting room. In the midst of death, scenes of everyday life constantly passed before us, and to such an indifference had our feelings been subdued that many of the students living at a distance thought nothing of taking sandwiches or light meals in this dissecting room, and washing all down with good porter clandestinely fetched by Paddy O'Rourke, the attendant on duty.

This Mr. Paddy O'Rourke was quite a character in his way, and a constant butt for the students, who played all manner of tricks on him, and worried his life out. He was a short and sturdy man, with a broad Irish face almost hidden in red whiskers; this face never being particularly clean, nor were his auburn locks often disturbed by brush or comb. He was decidedly ugly, full of droll sayings, being not only witty himself, but often the cause of that article being displayed by others.

In nowhere was he more amusing than when accompanying us on resurrection excursions to some of the neighbouring churchyards, his odd ideas and expressions often making a grave subject pass off in a scene of merriment. To hasten or frighten some of the younger students he kept perpetually repeating on these occasions, "Bedad, sir, they're coming," meaning the watch, or, "Faith, gentlemen, they are upon us now." We were not always successful in our search, and on one occasion when we were emptyhanded, Mr. O'Rourke proposed that we should play a trick on the watch themselves, so as to make them less observant in future.

We could not imagine what he was at, but when he spread out the two sacks which we usually carried with us, and suggested that two of us should for a time become occupants of these sacks, and, feigning to be dead, submit to being drawn on our car through some of the principal streets of the city, we were convulsed with laughter, and, entering into the joke, two of our number, first bargaining for some holes being cut in the top of the sacks for the admission of air, were duly packed up, and then drawn over Essex Bridge, of course lying stretched out as stiff as buckram.

The police or watchman saw something suspicious approaching, not in silence, however, but rather boisterously, and at once stayed our further progress. "Och! bedad, gintlemen, we are cotched, and sure hadn't we better give in dacently?" exclaimed Paddy, loud enough for the constables to hear, and who had taken possession of the car, at the same time directing us to go with them to the station, as engaged in body snatching

After a moment's dispute and a show of indignation on our part, two of the force got on the car and smoothly and in silence all went well enough until one of the occupants of the sacks sneezed. However, this appeared to pass unnoticed, but shortly afterwards one of the constables muttered something about a corpse moving, and whilst he was watching for a repetition of this unusual proceeding in a dead body, the other corpse was heard to groan distinctly, the occupant of the sack being nearly stifled through want of air. The constables becoming alarmed, and, like most of the peasantry, very superstitious, could not conceal their terror, and after whispering together, one exclaimed, trembling meanwhile like an aspen leaf, "Faith! they are coming to life again, and by the Holy Virgin it isn't for the loike of us to be here. We'd best be off and lave these body snatchers to take care of the craturs, dead or alive!"

No sooner said than done. They jumped off the car and scampered away in the dark, leaving Paddy O'Rourke and ourselves in uninterrupted enjoyment of the joke and its success. It was not until early next morning that we got home to the dissecting room, when Paddy exclaimed, "Bedad, gintlemen, I'll warrant them fellows won't interrupt us again in a hurry. Sure, there's fine times to come now."

Paddy habitually wore black; coat, breeches, waistcoat, and stockings, and these threadbare and seedy. He said that he preferred black as becoming his position in life, and he wore it, not as mourning for his wife recently deceased, whose death, he said, "was a great source of comfort, as she cost a lot in whisky," but in honour of the profession. Thus, must end the history of Paddy O'Rourke, the resurrectionist of Trinity College, Dublin.

I passed the winter very agreeably with my family in Dublin, seldom accepting invitations. Time was valuable, and I found dinner parties and entertainments unfitted me for work. A room in my mother's house was given me as a study, and here I worked hard, regularly, and steadily, having made up my mind to be a physician, and renounced agricultural pursuits; though still intent on marrying my cousin.

I was not sorry when the season arrived for my return to the University of Edinburgh, and early in spring I was travelling over the beaten path pursued last year, arriving in time to be present at the botanical lectures of Professor Rutherford, in which I became intensely interested, acquiring a fair knowledge of classification, and I also attended the midwifery course of Professor Hamilton.

CHAPTER 5

Attends Botanical Classes

Of course, I took leave of my cousin previous to quitting Dublin, but it was only by letter. In it I laid before her my future prospects, and hoping that someday I might claim her hand, begged her to write to me, directing at the Post Office in Edinburgh. The composition of that letter took me a long time, and I trusted it was so worded that a speedy and agreeable answer would result. However, I was doomed to disappointment, for a short time after my arrival at Edinburgh, and applying at the Post Office for letters, I found to my surprise that there was one for me, not from my charmer herself, but from her mother, an elderly lady whom I respected and feared, and whose writing I could have dispensed with.

She was very civil, but terribly practical, giving me to understand that I was far too "*boyish*" to think of matrimony, that an engagement with her daughter was out of the question, that I ought to pursue my studies, and that she should persuade my much-loved Jane to give up the affair.

I was not a little annoyed at the reference to my age—"boyish!" "A young man entering the medical profession" might have been more correct. Then the unfeeling way in which I was recommended to think no more of my goddess, but pursue my studies! However, in the word "persuade" there was hope. It showed that I was not altogether disregarded by the young lady, and that after all she might refuse to yield.

About a fortnight later I made another inquiry at the Post Office, and to my surprise and delight was handed a letter written by the fair Jane herself. Recognising the same, I hurried homewards the better to devour its contents in my own sitting-room; but I need not have so excited myself, had I opened it at the Post Office. The very first words sealed my fate. The dear girl made some acknowledgment of affection for me, but the mother's persuasion had been most effectual, inasmuch as she, too, thought an engagement most injudicious, and begged me no longer to consider her in any other light than that of a sincere friend, adding, in a postscript, that a reply was unnecessary.

Thus were all my hopes blasted. My air-built castles utterly demolished, and life was a blank. At any rate it was so for some time, until reason and reflection resumed their sway, when I began to think that perhaps after all it was for the best; so, I mustered up all the philosophy I could command, and gradually submitted to my fate. Of course, I sent no reply, the wretched postscript was too firmly written for doubt, and showed that the writer was in earnest. So ended my first love affair. Conceiving that I should be more independent in private lodgings than at a boarding-house, I took a couple of rooms well-furnished and for a reasonable rental at a tailor's in College Street, nearly opposite to the college gates.

The owners, Mr. and Mrs. Snip, promised to provide all that was requisite; and as they seemed to be good kind of people, I ventured to trust myself to their tender mercies for so long as I might find myself comfortable and things going satisfactorily. I found the old lady somewhat given to whisky, and her husband also inclined that way, but in a less degree. The woman thrived upon it, being stout, rubicund, and strong; but Mr. Snip did no credit to the drink, being yellow as a buttercup, and thinner than the thinnest of Pharoah's lean kine.

I might have availed myself more of the instruction in botany given in Dr. Rutherford's course, the Botanical Gardens where these lectures were delivered offering great advantages to students; but botany was not then considered interesting, nor so necessary as is the case now; but to me the want of a more complete knowledge of flowers, their classifications and their peculiarities, has been a subject of no small regret always.

I suspect young men are often led away from a necessary duty by the way, too often dull and uninteresting, in which many professors in our colleges deliver their lectures. The sense of honour as to the claims on their energies and knowledge of the subjects made by the colleges, and equally by the students, is often ignored or treated as not material. Only too many Professors hate the subjects for which they have been appointed to lecture and for which certain emoluments have been sanctioned. The fault of non-attendance by pupils is not altogether one-sided.

Doctor Hamilton, another professor, was very earnest, active, full of fun, and unusually interested in his duties. His manner and the real goodness of his lectures on midwifery, drew together a very great number of students. He was perhaps somewhat dogmatical in his opinions, looked with an air of the greatest contempt on those differing from him, and laid down the law with an emphatic thump on the table before him; as a consequence, he was constantly in hot water with some one or other of his *confrères*. Notwithstanding his peculiarities, we students felt very partial to him and allowed for his display of temper, well knowing that he was thoroughly up in his subject, and had a happy knack of communicating this knowledge to his hearers.

Perhaps some are yet in the flesh who remember the model made by this professor to be used at these lectures. It was ingenious and a good working model; however, had it failed, or even not been excellent; it would not have done to intimate this to the professor, his temper being violent. Indeed, it was said that at consultations he was most quarrelsome with those disagreeing with him in any form. He was quite a pigmy; but small men are often very pugnacious. A story was told how he and Gregory (a great raw-boned giant) almost came to blows in consequence of their disagreeing on a certain case before them. Dr. Gregory at length got so angry at the treatment received as to threaten the self-opinionated little man with giving him a seat on the hob of the fireplace, amidst the cordials and comforts there cooking for the use of the invalids.

The remainder of the summer I read very hard, and for a time I had to stop working, visiting the seaside, Roslyn Castle, Hawthornden, Dalkeith, Musselburgh, etc. etc., going no great distance from the city, as I endeavoured, if possible, to return to my solitary lodgings each night in College Street.

Towards the end of autumn students came to study medicine at Edinburgh from all parts of the globe. Indeed, at that time there was hardly a region on the surface of the civilised earth that did not furnish a quota of these students. The University was in the zenith of its fame, especially as regards the practice of medicine and the knowledge of chemistry; nevertheless, perfection was very far away, and carelessness not uncommon. Since the death of Munro, the anatomy students had decreased, and the lectures given by private practitioners in opposition to those held in the university, were listened to and appreciated by many who could not find sound and efficient instruction elsewhere.

Practical anatomy and dissections were not attended as well as formerly, the teaching was not good, and the great objection prevailing amongst the Scotch to necrotomy precluded research, and only too frequently prevented the investigation of causes which had resulted in the death of individuals; these individuals having been carried off suddenly, or dying from most interesting diseases. Hence our university at this time did very little for pathology.

A few subjects, as corpses were termed, served the professor for the session, and these mostly came from London, being often the cause of strange adventures to travellers. They were placed in sacks or hampers, and conveyed with other goods or even passengers by vans and coaches, or in Leith smacks; so that before they arrived at their destination many were in an advanced stage of decomposition, and if we were to judge by our own senses in the lecture-room, must have been highly odoriferous to their fellow-voyagers and travellers, more particularly in warm weather.

This being my last year at the university, and anxious to become better acquainted with the future of my profession, I inscribed my name on the books of Drs. Duncan, Gregory, and Holmes' classes besides becoming a pupil of the Royal Infirmary, with it obtaining the privilege of attending various other classes of instruction. In point of fact, I had more on my hands than I could well accomplish; and had I attended each class, there would have been no time for private study, which was almost as essential as public lectures,

I commenced with great fervour, rising long before daybreak, and studied very hard for the two hours preceding Dr. Holmes' lectures, which were held about eight o'clock, and on my return home, continued reading or in schools for the rest of the day. In fact, one way or another, between lectures, hospital practice, and private studies, I was more than fully occupied for ten or twelve hours each day, denying myself all gaieties and enjoyments, even necessary exercise, and somewhat overdid it; but I was anxious to get through the whole routine or curriculum of my medical education as quickly and economically as possible, though with credit to myself, and to put my widowed mother to no greater expenses than were unavoidable, for our means now were considerably diminished.

In those days it was a great object among the students to obtain the situation of clinical clerk, or to be an assistant to any of the professors whose turn it might be to deliver lectures at the Infirmary; being appointed was a compliment, and considered as an acknowledgment by the authorities of your skill and industry. I had applied to be so appointed both to Doctors Rutherford and Duncan, little expecting to obtain it, as the professor usually selected for it each term some friend from the more advanced students.

Judge, then, my surprise when many days and weeks had passed a message came to me from Doctor Rutherford, professor of botany and midwifery, saying that he had appointed me his clinical clerk for the ensuing quarter. I hardly knew how to act, and regretted my temerity in having applied. I felt convinced that I was not sufficiently advanced to fill the office effectually, having had little experience in treating disease. I was expected not only to write out concisely all cases for the professor, but to treat them until he was able to do this for himself. Altogether, I was afraid to encounter the office, and had all but given it up when I was advised by friends to accept, and to trust to what little knowledge I might possess, much to chance, and most to the professor's kindly nature, for success. I did so, and right glad I am, even now, that I got rid of my hesitation; for I found actual practice gave me a greater insight into disease than can be obtained by months of hard reading or attendance at lectures.

I was young, and can well remember the pleasure I experienced on being called upon to read aloud before the pupils assembled in the clinical wards the notes, I had made on the first case I had ever drawn up. At its conclusion the professor highly approved, and emphatically remarked, "Symptoms accurately described." The ice was broken, and after being some weeks in harness I think I did the work fairly well. The greatest difficulty I found was to write out in abbreviated Latin the prescriptions as dictated by Doctor Rutherford; but this I overcame, though, fortunately for me, the professor was not addicted to putting a *farrago* of medicines into his prescriptions—a fault somewhat common in the modern physician.

During the session I was a regular attendant at the meetings of the Royal Medical Society, where many excellent papers were read and discussed. These papers were written by the senior students, and given in according to the seniority of the student. Eventually it came to my turn; and the better to avoid discussion I selected a subject on which all were likely to agree, and consequently no one would be likely to contravene my statement as to its history and usual symptoms. Partly repenting, I told my idea to a fellow-countryman named Moore, who assured me that my paper should not be treated with silent contempt; and the better to ensure this, Moore rose directly my paper was read, and declared that the treatment of this disease was much better understood in olden times than at present, and cut up my views in such a way as necessitated a reply.

Moore went at me vigorously; sneeringly said "that the learned author was altogether wrong throughout his whole essay," and by some good jokes at my expense succeeded in keeping the society in a constant titter. After a while I had to reply, and did it *con amore*, making a regular onslaught on my opponent, saying that his ignorance was simply concealed in coarse jokes, and that I had no patience with his old-fashioned notions and milk-and-water treatment of such a disease, and the majority took my view of the subject.

At this society I formed the acquaintance of many men who in after life became well known in the profession; among others I may mention Sir H. Holland, Doctors Bright, Levy, Davy, Marshall Hall, etc. etc.; and I look back on the evenings spent there with great pleasure, though not unmixed with sorrow, as, alas! how many of them have departed this life? leaving behind them, nevertheless, glorious monuments of their talents, perseverance, and fame.

About this time, I received the gratifying intelligence from my dear uncle at Brighton, now knighted and appointed physician to the Court, that he had succeeded in obtaining for me from the authorities the promise of an assistant surgery in a cavalry regiment so soon as I should be qualified; and, as I hoped to take my degree in the following June, it left me but little time for preparation. I should have preferred deferring the degree until later on in the autumn, but my uncle had set his heart on my going up at midsummer; and so, if possible, I commenced reading harder than ever.

Thus, affairs passed until the spring, and as time was gaining on me quickly, I set about writing the usual thesis, which was to be done in the Latin language, according to the rules of the university. My subject was the influence of hot climates on European constitutions. This, of course, I first very carefully composed in English. The mere composition took time; but, obtaining information from known and reliable authorities, statistics, etc. etc., much longer. Books and references on this subject I found were rare and hard to obtain, and more than once I regretted having taken it up.

Wherefore I did so I now cannot remember; but days and weeks went by finding me hard at work, and well advanced in the translation. One night, when more than usually occupied over this thesis, my landlady handed me a note, which I found to be a summons to attend on a particular night, with my thesis, for a preliminary examination, to be held at Doctor Hope's house; and as no answer beyond acknowledging the receipt was required, I prepared accordingly. My feelings were none of the pleasantest. Vulgarly speaking, my heart was in my mouth, and I immediately commenced to anticipate all manner of horrors, ending in a complete failure.

That I should be plucked I felt assured; and, worst of all, remanded to my studies for another six months. The short time allowed me before this examination came off for finishing the thesis; and, proving to myself that I had a good general knowledge of the subjects in which I knew I should be tested did not improve my confidence or health. Hard study, mental anxiety, and sleepless nights do not conduce to bodily welfare.

I did not much fear the ordeal of an examination in the Latin language, or having to converse in it, as was then required; for I was a tolerably good scholar, had been well grounded, and read the classics for pleasure; but to encounter six learned professors, each and all asking you questions on subjects connected with medicine and affinities thereof, was rather much for my weak nerves; and more than once I felt inclined to shrink from the test, reporting myself insufficiently prepared. However, common-sense gained the mastery. I had either to appear or, by putting off my attendance until another opportunity, lose my army appointment, and which appointment I was particularly anxious to secure.

When the terrible day arrived, I was as nervous as an old woman, and could hardly tie my cravat, my hand shaking so abominably; but, donning my best, and accompanied by my friend Colquhoun, an American *confrère*, I knocked at Doctor Hope's door in Queen Street. Shown into a back sitting-room, I was left alone to ruminate: ample time for this pursuit being given me by the late arrival of the Professors. From Doctor Gregory not being on speaking terms with his brother Professor, I had supposed that he would not be present at an examination held in Doctor Hope's house. Indeed, the wish was father to the thought, for I feared Doctor Gregory's knowledge of the classics and his professional questions. My disappointment can be understood when, on my arrival in the room where the examination was to be held, the first object I saw was the portly figure of Professor Gregory.

I was politely invited to be seated, and the Professors forming a semicircle round me, Doctor Hope opened the ball by requesting me to fully describe the circulation of the blood. The question, put in Latin, was to be answered in that language. At that time this was, almost always, the first question put, and certainly a more important one could be with difficulty selected.

After I had once broken the ice, much of my nervousness departed, and I found the replying in Latin not a very difficult task. I spoke fairly, fluently, grammatically, and correctly, and more than once inwardly felt grateful for the good grounding I had obtained at school. The examination was close and thorough, each professor in his turn putting questions which, I think, would have exposed ignorance, had much of that existed. Of course, all the questions were not answered absolutely correctly; but as my nervousness wore away, and memory played her part, I felt I was doing far better than I expected.

After a lengthened time I was directed to retire, and, returning to the old sitting-room or parlour, had nothing for it but to hope that all would go well, and wait patiently for further orders.

Soon Doctor Hope made his appearance and heartily congratulated me on having passed a most satisfactory examination, praising me for close attendance to lectures and studies during the whole course I had been at the university, and especially commending my knowledge of the classics, adding, "So pleased are the professors with the knowledge you have exhibited, that they sanction your sending your thesis at once to the press for publication."

Of course, I was highly delighted and greatly surprised. After thanking Doctor Hope and his brother professors for their kindness and consideration, I took my leave, and with a light step and yet lighter heart rejoined my friend Colquhoun, who had waited for me the long while in a neighbouring tavern.

The permission to print your thesis was well known among the students as meaning that all future ordeals would be trifling; the first examination, in fact, being the criterion of a man's proficiency. This may or may not be a good plan, but it seemed to answer at Edinburgh. It certainly gave a young fellow confidence, and the examination being close, on various subjects, and by six or more men having no particular leaning towards a single individual, was not likely to favour ignorance; but the system of holding an examination at a brother professor's house is wrong and open to abuse.

The use of Latin for colloquial purposes tells on all not well grounded in the classics; but the physician as a man of science, and associating most probably with the higher and better educated classes, should not be inferior to any of these in higher attainments. There were several degrees of facility in the use of this language among the professors but Doctor Gregory was pre-eminently superior to them all, using it with as much ease as his own native tongue, and with a degree of elegance for which he was remarkable.

Having passed the preliminary examination, I somewhat relaxed in my studies. This indeed I felt was necessary. Symptoms, not altogether desirable, caused by over work and want of exercise, occasionally exhibiting themselves; so, I once again mixed in society and received no little hospitality from many of the residents. The Dingwalls, Kirks, and other old families were particularly hospitable, and through them my invitations were many. It kept me from the temptations of a college life. Late suppers, theatres, and little dinners often lead to drinking and other vices, and create a dislike to professional labour; indeed, only too often the want of stability first finds a root in a college supper or tavern bout,

A married woman with good tact, and by advice, influence, and offering sociability can be the means of keeping many young men from bad company and worse habits. Thanks to kind friends, I never was tempted during my whole long stay at the university to associate with the dissipated or enter inferior society. I found no difficulty in being amused elsewhere. I was of opinion then, am so still, and that at the end of a life of experiences of many sorts, that the want of success of many men at college, in professions, and indeed in everyday business, is only too frequently their own faults. Idleness and want of self-respect are common causes, make what excuses they may or their friends may for them.

I was somewhat curtailed in these amusements by Doctor Duncan appointing me clinical clerk at the hospital; he having succeeded Doctor Rutherford in the routine of that duty. Of course, I accepted the appointment; the compliment in being asked to take it was great, and the experience gained therein greater, though my having to quit the university in June limited these advantages.

The 24th of June was the day fixed for my final examination before obtaining the degree of M.D.; but I was constantly called upon to write out various cases on medical subjects, to translate and explain passages from Hippocrates, Galen, and other authors, and to furnish documents connected with my office; so, I found plenty of occupation, and felt all the better for the variety.

At the appointed time we students were all assembled in the large library of the university, probably one hundred of us. It was a serious time for us; our future may be said to commence from that date. Of these young men a fair number would soon be sent on their mission *hic et ubique terrarium,* to practice the noble art of medicine, or, as has been satirically remarked, to have a licence to kill any amount of His Majesty's subjects.

There was a very large assembly of doctors and the outside public, both male and female, all anxious to witness the proceedings and capping of their friends or relatives, as also to hear how well or ill we could defend our thesis, or explain away errors in composition or judgment. Professor Gregory took up mine and asked me some abominably tight questions, finally complimenting me in Latin on its composition. So on with others, when finally, the principal of the university rose up, moving forward, and was followed by the various professors.

Then the principal touched the head of each of us students who had passed, with the black velvet cap in his hand, at the same time saying some Latin words, which same words have now slipped my memory. The professors following shook the successful one by the hand, congratulating him on the event, and each was dubbed a "Doctor," *Summos in Medecina honores.* I candidly own I felt supremely delighted, and at once held my head somewhat higher. It seemed as if the game of life had now begun, and I trust that I was not ungrateful to God for having brought me thus far upon the threshold of independence, to be the forerunner of my own fortunes, and for the prospect of being no longer a tax on the very limited income of my widowed mother.

Doubtless the situation was shared in by a large number of my brother students. How few looked forward with anything but a bright eye to the future! How few dreaded failure in the onward path of life! In fact, all were buoyant, anxious to lose no time in entering upon their new course with alacrity, and hoping, each in his several sphere, to reach the temple of fame, and at some future date to find themselves illustrious!

To the few of us now remaining what is the sense of our feelings? Is it a subject of disappointment or of congratulation? Having obtained my degree, I felt bound to give a dinner to some few of my most intimate friends, the majority of whom were among the newly dubbed Doctors. It was a pleasant evening, speeches, whisky toddy, and mutual congratulations caused us to enjoy ourselves amazingly. It was my farewell to the University of Edinburgh.

CHAPTER 6

Quits the University

A few days after this, and bidding farewell to many, many kind friends made, I left Edinburgh for London, putting myself on board a Leith smack. The weather was boisterous, and it was not until the fourth day of a very rough passage that we arrived in the Thames. It was all rough—ship, weather, sea, food, and men; but it was well I started when I did, as the bad weather continued, indeed, became worse, and a longer detention would have added starvation to the many miseries.

As it was through Doctor Bankshead that my uncle had obtained for me the appointment of assistant-surgeon in the cavalry, I made a point of losing no time in paying my respects to him; and being a countryman of my own, and withal a most hospitable man, I was immediately asked to dinner, it being arranged that next day I should accompany him to the Director General of the Army Medical Board so as to take up my commission, and ascertain what my duties were. The handsome doctor was most kind and attentive to me, asked about all his old haunts in Edinburgh, where he had been a contemporary with my uncle, and kept me till a late hour talking over old times, old scenes, and old acquaintances.

Doctor Bankshead was certainly a most agreeable man. His looks and manners were so fascinating that he made his way at once among the aristocracy, though considerably indebted to Lord Carrington for introductions, his lordship being in command of the Militia regiment of which Bankshead was surgeon. Resigning this appointment, the doctor commenced practice in London. Fortune favoured him; good looks and agreeable manners stood him in better stead than very great talents. He was no reader, nor was he a close observer on professional subjects. However, this fashionable son of Escalapius was a sincere and kind friend to me.

Under his auspices, the next day I attended at the Medical Board, and the Director General informed me that before I could be gazetted, I must pass the College of Surgeons. This was a new view of matters. It had never been mentioned to me before as necessary, and I supposed the examinations passed in anatomy, etc. etc., at Edinburgh would have sufficed. However, there was no help for it; and as latterly I had somewhat neglected surgical subjects, I was not prepared to appear immediately before the Board of Examiners, but saw the necessity for resuming my reading with unabated vigour for at least a fortnight. Taking a lodging off Holborn, I set to work at surgery, *con amore,* endeavouring to brush up anything I had forgotten or was doubtful upon.

It was very severe study indeed that I forced upon myself, and I had cause to regret that during the past year at Edinburgh I had allowed the subject of surgery to be neglected, though I hardly see how I could have found time for that and the studies in medicine I had taken up. The strain on my system was too much, and in a few weeks after passing the College of Surgeons I completely broke down, being seized with a horrible distemper, known as "sweating sickness," which almost brought me to death's door.

I succeeded in passing the College of Surgeons "most creditably." There were many examiners and perhaps thirty or forty students to be examined. Various questions, some very intricate, were put to the students, and success or failure in the reply at once noted. Then after a while each examiner took one or two students for closer examination, noting the replies as before. I was consigned to the tender mercies of a chirurgical and very eccentric knight then in great fame. He took me on a great number of subjects; and, strange to say, on the treatment of most of the cases he suggested we entirely disagreed. I had been taught otherwise.

I soon discovered that the worthy knight had his own crotchets upon almost everything; but in the end we got on famously. With a smile he observed, as I stuck to my teaching, "Yes, young gentleman, you answer perfectly correctly as you have been taught in the schools, but on the field of battle and in most cases, if you will adopt my plans, you will do much better."

The diploma described me as qualified for "Full Army Surgeon," and as in many instances this position was gazetted, I hoped it might be so in my case; but I was appointed to serve as assistant surgeon. However, about all this I knew nothing; I paid a larger sum in fees for the exalted position which I did not obtain. In a few days I received my commission as "Hospital Assistant to His Majesty's Forces" from the Horse Guards, and was directed to report myself to the Senior Medical Officer at the York Hospital, Chelsea. This accordingly I did, finding myself immediately put into harness, and had to take lodgings in the town, and to learn that not improbably it would be some time before I should be appointed to a cavalry regiment as assistant surgeon.

It was in the year 1813 that I first commenced my military career, and I found myself something like a fish out of water among the comical set of fellows I met with at the York Hospital. Physicians, staff-surgeons, hospital assistants, apothecaries, and the queer lot generally, composing the staff of a general hospital. The principal medical officer was a stout, jolly looking Irishman, who somehow had obtained his position without having previously occupied any of the inferior grades—not very fair on those in the service before him, and many of whom were serving at this time before the enemy.

At the hospital there were two or three staff surgeons, under whose orders the assistants acted. These did their duties efficiently and systematically, one being always officer of the day, and consequently never quitted the hospital on the day of duty, so as to be prepared to receive any sent in wounded or seriously ill.

This duty came round disagreeably often; of course, the confinement to the hospital walls was monotonous enough, but it was the bad commons and disgusting bedding which tried one most. "The Ordinary," or, as it would now be termed, "Hospital Mess," was very bad. Our pound of beef was anything in the shape of meat, and as tough as shoe leather; the potatoes bad and badly boiled; one pound of bread of the brickbat nature; and a pint of porter sufficiently sour to necessitate our practising on ourselves the cure for diarrhoea; as for the bedding it was damp and dirty, with sheets so coarse as to act like nutmeg graters.

It might have been disagreeable, this duty, but it gave us a good insight into practice, and brought us into contact with all manner of characters among the soldiers who from time to time became the inmates of the hospital. Some of them were really good, brave, and heroic fellows, who submitted to every kind of treatment and operation with undaunted courage; but others were most obstinate and discontented, using every kind of dodge to impose upon us young doctors, and to avoid being sent back to duty.

To this end, some even of the younger soldiers, benefiting by the instruction given to them by old malingerers, caused sores and slight wounds, which under ordinary circumstances would have healed quickly, to become inflamed and daily worse. Tongues rubbed against the whitewashed walls certainly puzzled us doctors. Fits were common and constantly enacted in the barrack yard, lameness was a general complaint, and not a few declared themselves to be hopelessly paralysed.

Of this being "hopelessly paralysed" a ludicrous instance presented itself one day. One old malingerer told young Bancroft, the then medical officer of the day, that he "was without sensation or capability of motion," and added that all power had deserted his limbs. To this very serious state of things young B. thought it right to call our attention, declaring it to be a very accurate example of Cullen's nosological distinction of palsy; and, suspecting the fellow, he coolly took out of a tray a little piece of live charcoal, used for softening plaisters, with his forceps, and at once applied it to the paralysed limb of the shamming soldier.

The fellow, unsuspecting and taken by surprise, jumped up from his bed with a yell, and with execrations loud and deep, scampered about the ward, totally forgetful of his former asseverations as to the nature of the dreadful disease from which he suffered. Being thus self-detected, his return to regimental duty was speedily effected.

After I had been about six weeks at the York Hospital, I was seized with severe illness, night sweats, and great debility. I was too ill to perform any duties, and the Director-General gave me unlimited sick leave of absence, recommending my going down to Brighton, and gave me to understand that probably there would be some difficulty now in my obtaining the assistant surgency in the cavalry regiment having the vacancy; nevertheless, if I wished it, he would endeavour to procure for me the same appointment in another cavalry regiment. The particular regiment mattered little to me, but this was unknown to the Director-General.

The truth was, an assistant surgeon of hussars had applied for an exchange into a regiment quartered in the north; and, knowing that I should be posted in his room, hoped to receive something from me towards meeting his expenses in the exchange; but, finding that I did not intend giving him one *sou*, he changed his mind, and withdrew his application. Meanwhile, I found myself gazetted as assistant surgeon to the regiment of Dragoon Guards at that time quartered at Edinburgh.

My health soon improved at Brighton under my kind uncle's care; and, just as I had made preparations to join the Dragoon Guards at

41

Edinburgh, I was informed that my friend of the hussars had again applied for an exchange, and the result was my removal to the 15th Hussars, but where serving or quartered I was not informed. However, I was not kept long in ignorance, for in a day or two the post brought me an official letter at my uncle's house, where I was staying, requesting me to report myself without delay to the officer commanding the cavalry depot at Brighton, adding that, "as there was a paucity of medical officers, he would feel obliged by my joining before the expiration of my sick leave, if possible." Of course, I had only to obey, and next day presented myself at the quarters of the officer commanding the depot, but in plain clothes, as we doctors were not supposed to get uniform until finally posted.

The colonel received me very graciously. He was acquainted with many of my relatives; and, after introducing me to many of the officers, doing duty at the depot, took me down to the hospital, and at once installed me in office. These duties were not very arduous, there being very few on the sick list, and these but trifling cases; besides, I found the hospital sergeant a most intelligent fellow, as capable of mixing up drugs as any apothecary's apprentice. Altogether, Sergeant Bolland was a very superior man, intelligent, good-looking, and uncommonly stout, showing that he lived more upon the fat of the land than on the physic under his care. He had the supplying of all extras required for the sick, and doubtless made a very good thing by it.

I was the guest of the colonels at mess that evening, where, besides our own officers, were many others belonging to regiments attached to the depot. The conversation was more lively than improving—somewhat of shop, but more about the pretty girls of Brighton. Not being accustomed to this style, it became rather monotonous, it being clear that the fair sex and horses monopolised the chief part of my brother officers' thoughts and ideas. The lieutenants and cornets were terrible lady-killers. I must make exception from among the older hands, who had seen a great deal of service, and were now full of the things happening every day in the war going on in the Peninsula, and they unable to take part therein.

There was not much wine drunk, and after dinner I accepted the invitation of Captain Carpenter to coffee in his quarters. He, finding that I was a flute player, wished me to join him in a duet, which, doubtless, was executed to our mutual advantage and satisfaction. I spent a very pleasant evening, and Carpenter and I became great friends, continuing such for many years.

Captain Carpenter had been a long time in the service, and had seen some hard fighting, and as a man was a general favourite, but not thought much of as an officer, being too fidgety and too quiet. He never neglected his duties, nor was in any way deficient in a knowledge of his profession; but he cared not for excitement, which, with the routine of duties, constituted the very existence of army life among the officers of those days. He neither hunted, shot, gambled, nor drank wine freely, and was very ignorant on the good points of a horse. He was beyond the general run of officers in accomplishments, knowing the classics well, and several foreign languages, though not a university man; good-looking, and, as one may imagine, not a little admired by the fair sex. He was a perfect gentleman.

I had hardly joined when the depot of the regiment was transferred to the Arundel Barracks—a disappointment to me, as I had hoped to have remained some time longer among my relatives, and to have more fully enjoyed the festivities then going on at Brighton. However, it is not for soldiers to cavil or grumble at orders, and away we marched; but, as I was unprovided with uniform and charger, I was permitted to travel by coach to the new quarters.

We occupied the wooden huts erected as temporary barracks outside the town, and tried to be comfortable. Our mess consisted of about a dozen officers, but two of these being married, were not expected to dine very frequently. It was rather expensive altogether. Riches are certainly useful articles, but probably were neither more nor less necessary for cavalry officers in those days than they are in the present. Poverty may do very well for poets to rave about or sing praises thereon, but it was not a thing much esteemed at cavalry messes. To shirk expense was decidedly disapproved of, and I give one instance occurring to myself.

I had been feeling very ill, and especially so when one evening at mess a young lieutenant asked me to take wine with him; but to his surprise and that of the whole table I begged to decline, on the plea that I was feeling unwell; he and others, thinking that I was feigning ill-health by way of avoiding expense. However, such was not my motive, as I was really ill, and in a day or two had to take to my room, where I was detained for a long period; but the first man to call and to inquire after me, and indeed to be most attentive, was this young lieutenant whose invitation to wine had created an unjust suspicion.

Luckily, there were few sick in hospital, for a substitute for me was not or could not be found. Sergeant Bolland for some time was the only means of communication between the patients and myself, and between us we did the duties fairly well; but I improved by degrees, very slowly I allow. My illness was great and hard to shake off; indeed, when I was called upon to inspect medically two troops ordered to leave Portsmouth and join the headquarters of the regiment serving in the Peninsula, I felt so unwell as to be almost unable to perform the duty.

I applied to accompany these, and should have been sent had not this attack of illness occurred; as it was, I had sole charge of the depot, as the medical authorities in London had no medical officers available for my relief. All those about to depart for the seat of war were in high glee, and such was the anxiety of the colonel to make a good muster, that he actually sent out several horses under five years of age and some men little better than raw recruits, both ill adapted for campaigning in winter. The departure of my friend Carpenter was annoying, even more so to me than being left at the depot. I felt that sooner or later my turn must come; but I knew very little of the officers remaining behind, and they the same of me.

I saw the whole marched out of the barrack yard in a snow storm, and could not help asking myself how many of these, think ye, will ever return? For at this time no one expected the Peninsular War would so soon terminate, and that with the *éclat* it eventually did.

The depot was left under the command of Captain John Bull, an old officer of great experience and much respected by his superiors. He had risen from the ranks, having served in the Egyptian campaign with an infantry regiment as a sergeant, and had by bravery and good conduct risen to his present position. Of course, his inability to purchase caused him to be frequently passed over for promotion by his more wealthy juniors; but Old Bull, as he was termed, took the thing quite philosophically, and consoled himself with an extra bottle of port, a wine he admired much. Indeed, this and attachment to the fair sex were Old Bull's peculiarities, and in these, more especially in the first, he indulged more than was good for edification or example to the young officers constantly joining the depot.

However, we were not overstocked with cornets, for our colonel kept the patronage of these appointments entirely to himself, resisting the efforts of the Horse Guards to foist their *protégés* upon him.

Old Bull was terribly afraid of this colonel, who usually resided in London. Gossip said that the riding-master and quartermaster kept the colonel well informed of all that went on at the depot, thus accounting for Old Bull's civility to these individuals, excusing them from all parades, expecting from them nothing but the barest performance of their respective duties, and often inviting them to become his guests at mess, thus entailing a share of their entertainment expenses to fall on other officers. Von Prank, the riding-master, was a *protégé* of the colonel, and whether he did as was supposed, I know not. He had been appointed by the colonel, and was a good-hearted fellow.

Von Prank gave pleasant little supper parties, the food consisting, for the most part, of the fish caught in our small river. The usual drink was some excellent cognac, smuggled in by certain adepts at the game, said to be consigned to the quartermaster. It was no affair of Old Bull's. He drank the brandy, purchased it, and asked no questions.

Many of us were given to fishing, and only too often on our return to the barracks we turned into the Bridge Hotel, winding up the evening with a dinner and wine. It was a foolish proceeding, and chiefly because the daughters of the hostess were pretty, and we could talk soft nonsense to them. These girls knew half the officers of the army, as they were always billeted on their mother's house when regiments marched through, although it was not the leading inn of the place. It was presumed that the old lady had some interest with the head constable, and the daughters offered great attractions.

One way or another, these Scots got a good deal of money out of us officers, which more legitimately ought to have been spent in our own mess; but as the neighbourhood was very inhospitably inclined, and as our commanding officer set us the example, we were only too often visitors at the Bridge Hotel.

Several cornets joined us as summer came on, and among them were some queer fellows. In their own estimation, as a rule, they were very great men, had had much experience, and knew the world thoroughly. One, the son of a Scotch baronet, gave himself insufferable airs. Like most Scotchmen, he was well educated, and soon found out the weak points of our commanding officer, who, to be sure, with the exception of professional, was on every subject supremely ignorant.

The new cornet was very fond of getting into an argument, talked big about his ancestors (a class of beings little valued by Old Bull, who, as the maker of his own fortune, cared not a rush from what grade in life a man had sprung, provided he was honest and willing to do his duty), and made himself universally disagreeable. Shirking duty was our cornet's weakness, and this being discovered, Old Bull gave him an extra share, a remedy not relished, but the cornet had to obey, and might grumble to his heart's content.

Another young gentleman, according to his own account, was not only the greatest lady-killer ever known, but an equally great duellist; at once terrible in love and war. His tales were numerous and exhibited great courage and decision on his part. Once, he said, he had been under the disagreeable necessity of calling his own father out, but the matter ultimately was settled without fighting. "A most unusual occurrence," he observed, adding, "This duelling to me has been the cause of many a wound received and given."

One night a droll old captain sitting opposite to this fire-eating cornet at dinner, was asked by one of us the reason for his being in so meditative a mood, as he was observed to be unusually silent, and to do little else than look towards the window to which the cornet's back was placed.

The captain, as if awaking from a reverie, sharply replied, "I was only trying to see the stars through the numerous bullet holes in our cornet's body."

The cornet coloured and would have blustered, but became subdued, and eventually was jocular at the expense of Von Prank, the riding-master; but he lost by the game, inasmuch as at riding-school Von Prank caused him to take equestrian instruction upon the roughest young horse in the depot, and exercise on horseback not being a source of pleasure to the young fellow our cornet's happiness was but short-lived. Soon after the cornet left the regiment, but not before we had marched from Arundel barracks to join headquarters.

During the summer the Battle of Toulouse having finished the war, many regiments returned to England, the 15th Hussars among others, and we got a sudden order to march to Hounslow, there to join the headquarters of the regiment on their arrival from France; through the length of which country, they were to march previously to embarking for England. Grand fellows! They had indeed seen hard fighting, and had served their country well.

Leaving Arundel was to me no sorrow. It was inhospitable, monstrous dull, and I being young, naturally wished to see something more of the world than was to be found here; but my joy was not quite unalloyed, and I felt very uneasy on one point, it being reported that economy was to be the order of the day, and now that peace was concluded with France, the strength of the regiment would be reduced, and I, being junior of my rank, would be sent to the right-about and placed on half-pay; a position I was not by any means anxious to re-

15th Hussars officer and troopers

alise. However, as events afterwards turned out, I had no real cause for apprehension.

We had a very pleasant march, the weather being most enjoyable, and among the older hands all was joy at the prospect of again meeting old comrades, and hearing from them a narration of adventures and battles in Spain and France; for the regiment had highly distinguished itself, and was conspicuous among the many who had done honour to themselves and their country, both as regards discipline and bravery.

At Uxbridge there was a very jolly meeting; very many of the officers who had recently landed from France riding over across country, so as to greet old friends. It was a heavy night at mess, more than one practical joke being played. Our duelling cornet was in great feather, and somewhat astonished the officers who had lately arrived from abroad by his tales and boastings.

The cornet made himself unusually ridiculous on this occasion, becoming confidential and regretting that hitherto his hunting for an heiress had been unsuccessful; but few cared to be bored by him, and as I was still weak and suffering from illness, I excused myself from remaining very long at mess, and had retired to lie down on the sofa in the next room, where all was darkness and quiet. After a while the cornet entered, evidently in search of something he had left there, and a sudden thought struck me that I might play a trick on my bouncing friend. Knowing the kind of man, he was, I assumed a feigned voice, and after apologising for taking possession of his brother officer's ante-room for a few minutes, I informed him that I was only waiting until another apartment could be prepared for myself and only daughter, for whose health I was now travelling.

Then I entered into general conversation with him, answering his numerous questions, pretending not to see the drift of them, and appearing to be most trusting and confiding. I told him that the dear child had long been out of health. She was an only daughter, good, and beautiful, but I asked, "What availed the wealth I had created if it were to pass away to others than my own flesh and blood?" The bait took; our cornet became extremely sympathetic, trusted that the young lady's illness was not so serious as I had intimated, and hoped I would allow him to pay his respects to this daughter, making her acquaintance. Obtaining this much, he asked me if I should like to be introduced to his brother officers, who were having their wine in the next room.

Before consenting, I begged to be informed as to whom it might

48

CORNET, 15TH HUSSARS, 1820's

be I was addressing, and the answer being most satisfactory I accepted his kind offer. He told me that he was a captain commanding one of the troops belonging to the cavalry which that day had entered the town, and that his family were wealthy and highly connected. This settled, the distinguished officer quitted the apartment to prepare the officers for the introduction, which he trusted would be allowed.

The cornet told the officers that in a most extraordinary manner he had become acquainted with an old gentleman lying on the sofa in the other room, who had made him aware of all his family circumstances. This old gentleman evidently was very ill, but had a beautiful daughter, an only child, who would inherit all his wealth, for the old fellow was enormously rich. To an introduction to this daughter the father had consented, and marry her he certainly would.

The officers expressed surprise, and not a few doubted, knowing the propensity our cornet had for stretching the long bow. However, he stopped all cavilling by asking them to come and judge for themselves, adding: "The old gentleman expressed a desire to make your acquaintance." A general move was made, and snatching up the candles, all came tumbling into the room, where "the poor old gentlemen seemed to be coughing his very life out." The *éclaircissement* was soon made when the assistant-surgeon was found to be the sick man on the sofa.

A shout of laughter explained the imposition practised upon the lovesick cornet, and soon after this he exchanged into another regiment. A few days after this we joined the headquarters of the regiment, which had arrived at Hounslow, and old friends met old friends, battles were fought over again, and many a history told of bravery and death on the field of victory. It had been stirring times for those in the army serving abroad. Napoleon and his generals gave us full employ; but the wholesale slaughter and constant defeats at last made the French see that they were beaten, and that glory could be too highly purchased even were it obtained.

Allowing a short time for brushing-up, we were then reviewed by the Prince Regent, the Duke of Wellington, and the commander-in-chief, who expressed themselves as highly satisfied with our drill and discipline. Then our strength was reduced to eight troops, and we were ordered to proceed to Ireland. After so long a war, so much fighting, and so much knocking about, many of the men were glad to avail themselves of pensions; but the reduction was a sad blow to the hopes of many of the officers. Some of them were placed on half-pay, and

OFFICER, 15TH HUSSARS, 1820's

sorrowful indeed was the parting between comrades. For many years they had lived together, shared privations, hardships, and dangers; the regiment was the only home they knew, and now this was broken up.

In more respects than one the partings resembled the wrench to family ties caused by marriage, death, or certain incidents occurring in everyday life. In regiments, as in families, oftentimes the strongest affections are generated, and the necessary separation is seldom unaccompanied by the sad thought that the parting is for ever, the probability of again meeting being distant, and that a new style of life must be commenced, which will bring with it none of the good fellowship and unselfish kindness found in the regimental home. The necessity for the reduction of the strength of all regiments and lessening expenses to taxpayers was only too obvious. We had not only done almost all the fighting, but the greater part of the paying, and now that Napoleon was an exile, and the peace bringing with it universal joy and happiness, promising to be of long duration, of course the country demanded economy.

The French apparently were satisfied with their new king, though for how long seemed doubtful, with a nation so frivolous and never knowing their own minds two minutes together; it was nevertheless a period of anxiety. Our reward for all this bloodshed and expenditure was small enough. We had done our duty and got small thanks for the same. The nations for whom all this sacrifice had been made, and to rescue whom from the yoke of Napoleon we had gone and done so much, helped us hardly at all, and, to say the least of it, appeared to be monstrous ungrateful.

We were ordered to march to Liverpool, whence we were to embark for Ireland, a country evidently not much appreciated by the regiment; but few if any knew much about Ireland, and since its embodiment the Fifteenth had never been quartered there. With the exception of two of the officers, myself and another, all were natives of Great Britain, and if I am not mistaken, not a single non-commissioned officer or trooper hailed from the Emerald Isle.

The colonel had a strange dislike to Irishmen. Recruiting parties were never sent to Ireland, so nothing was known about Paddy's good qualities; but rather a prejudice existed against him, from the colonel downwards; however, in after years this feeling ceased to exist. Nay! even a few Papists were admitted into the ranks, a proceeding which would have almost disturbed the very bones of our late colonel, then mouldering in the grave, had he known of the dreadful fact.

In this long march I was peculiarly happy and fortunate in being attached to my dear friend Carpenter's squadron, that officer having returned uninjured. He set his face against all extravagance in the mess or in any way, of course not entirely to the satisfaction of many whose means were ample. To me it was decidedly advantageous, as in those days there was no marching allowance, and our bills could be made very expensive. Thanks to Carpenter, ours were light, but would have been lighter had Old Bull, whose troop was attached to the squadron, been less fond of port wine, and caused us to share the expense.

In those days most of the waiters in country inns were an unsophisticated lot, and blundered over their work abominably. I must be excused for telling this short anecdote of one attending on us at Warrington, Old Bull had ordered the mess dinner, and just as the cloth was laid, he told the waiter to bring in a bottle of their best port wine. "Remember, my man, not to decant it, but bring it up in the black bottle," he added.

"Yes, sir," replied the waiter, disappearing, and returning quickly, carrying the precious bottle most carelessly under his arm. Observing this, one of the officers cried out: "That's the way to do it. Shake it well, my man." When, no sooner said than done, and away went the waiter,' shaking the bottle lustily, much to Old Bull's horror and our amusement.

"Take it back, you fool, and be more careful with the next. Port wine isn't physic requiring to be well shaken before taking," roared Old Bull, purple with rage.

The waiter obeyed. He had learned a lesson, but it had a bad effect on his spirits and capacities. He was much depressed and blundered exceedingly.

At Warrington we were detained upwards of a week, as the transports for conveying us across the Channel had not arrived at Liverpool, but we enjoyed the delay. The gentry round were civil to us, and hospitable.

Among others Mr. B——, very well known throughout the county, showed us the greatest attention, giving a grand ball in our honour, rendered doubly pleasant by the attendance of most of the neighbouring ladies. Among these few equalled our host's charming daughters, one of whom afterwards became a princess by marrying an impecunious foreigner, for which privilege a small fortune was paid by her friends. Ah! well! I hope it turned out all right; but I often wonder how the fair daughters of England dare the risk, and so often ally

53

themselves with these mushroom nobility, when their own country contains so many men of superior ancestry, position, and wealth.

CHAPTER 7

Quarters at Kilkenny

At last, we arrived at Liverpool, and found the transports all ready, and in due course of time—an abominably rough passage—we entered the far-famed and beautiful bay of Dublin, just after the sun had risen, which threw a glorious refulgence upon all the surrounding scenery. The sight was more than beautiful, it was enchanting, and I hoped that it would make some impression on my comrades, and tend to lessen their prejudice against my ill-fated country. Whether it did so or not I could not ascertain; they certainly were not so impressed with the sight as myself, and I am afraid the beauties were lost upon them.

On landing, we were informed that the regiment was to proceed at once to the south, a disappointment to us all, more especially to myself, who fondly hoped to be quartered in Dublin, where my family lived, and in the neighbourhood of which I had many relatives. All I could get was a short leave of absence, and at its termination had to join my squadron at Kilkenny. Time flew past very quickly and pleasantly, and at the expiration of my leave I rejoined at Kilkenny, where I was quartered with Captain Leeds, a great, tall Yorkshireman, not perhaps a very enlightened individual, but a capital judge of a horse, and a most inveterate murderer of the King's English. Between "'osses, 'ounds, and 'unting," he was a great source of amusement to the boys of Kilkenny, where a very good pack of foxhounds was kept and where, of course, horses and hunting were very common topics of conversation.

At first the Irishmen did not understand very well the Yorkshireman's lingo; but, when they did comprehend what he meant, many were the traps set to catch him on his favourite subject; and at times it was almost impossible to keep one's countenance when he took the bait and floundered among the H's, sometimes swallowing it at a gulp, and then thrusting it forward when not wanted. The Irish at any rate are not prone to make these mistakes; indeed, they have rather a weakness in the opposite direction; but the good folk of Kilkenny, as also those of Limerick, have a notion that they speak the English language far more purely than the English themselves.

This may be, for our well of English is terribly defiled; but the constant repetition of the words "Ah, now," "Indeed, sure," "'Pon my honour and word," however sweet they may sound from the lips of the pretty lasses of Limerick (and they are indeed pretty), leads some to think that after all the inhabitants of Kilkenny and Limerick may be mistaken.

Many of the nobility and gentry in the neighbourhood called, as also the leading gentry of the place, among these Mr. H———m, the well-known banker. He had quite a brilliant *duodecimo* in the way of a pretty daughter, who was talkative and agreeable, and by no means averse to the company of our gallant Yorkshireman. I remember, on one occasion, when she accompanied our tall and somewhat awkward captain to the esplanade, where the band of the 42nd Highlanders was performing, the tune being "The Bold Dragoon," when some wicked wags immediately began to sing the words, "*Now he was tall and slim, she squat and short had grown*," to the no small merriment and full appreciation of all the lookers-on, as the application was irresistible. Indeed, the captain was so put out by this specimen of Irish wit, that he took uncommonly good care not again to encounter the jokes of the boys of Kilkenny, by being seen with the old banker's daughter.

The 42nd prided themselves on their pipers, and once, when dining at their mess, I was quite startled by the sudden blast of the bagpipes behind me, as the pipers poured forth martial airs, and marched round the mess table on the cloth being removed.

To the natives of Scotland, it may have been charming, and to the soldiers, they say, the tones of the bagpipes are most exhilarating; but to me the sound is barbaric and horrible, and I was glad when the *sans-culotted* Highlanders took their departure. Of the two dreadful instruments of music, I prefer the Irish pipes, or, rather, dislike them least: they are not so noisy, nor are they accompanied by that perpetual drone so soothing to the mind of a Scotchman, However, one must not judge national peculiarities: a Scotchman gets excited over the noise of his bagpipes, thinking it music; the Hindoo does the same over his tom-tom, and the Savoyard in the grinding of a hurdy-gurdy.

I remained but a short time at Kilkenny, as I was directed to take medical charge of the squadron quartered at Feathard, under the command of Captain Alexander, an old Peninsular officer, rather a martinet, and at heart a good fellow, but not particularly polished or educated, having risen from the ranks. He had but few resources beyond hunting and trying to fish or shoot, with now and then an excess after dinner in the drinking way. He then became quarrelsome, and, being a man of great courage and self-appreciation, only too often got mixed up in personal disputes, and would lay wagers to perform feats on horseback requiring great skill and nerve, and was always quite ready to eat the man daring to doubt his capabilities.

There were some nice families in the town and neighbourhood, with whom I became very intimate, and whose society I very much enjoyed. We officers made parties with them to see the sights in the country, visiting, among other places, the ruins of the castle of Cashel; and whilst wandering over these ruins I could not help wondering whether so much destruction was the work of time, or the conqueror's revenge. Alas! poor Ireland. She was not thus in days gone by. Will she ever regain her former splendour? I trow not.

Notwithstanding the hospitality and kindness of all around, it was often no easy matter to kill time at Feathard. To be sure, our headquarters were only a few miles away, at Clonmel, where we sometimes rode over to dine, or join in at the balls and parties given by the inhabitants, who were civil and extremely attentive to a select few of us; but, as a rule, these great attentions did not receive the consideration they might have deserved. Our officers, as being all English, and, with few exceptions, well born and fairly well off, were considered as good speculations in the matrimonial department by scheming mammas, and perhaps so by their pretty daughters; but ours were not marrying men, and. as I said before, had a prejudice against Ireland and the Irish. Indeed, amongst the whole of us but one officer married during the period we were quartered in Ireland.

However, great were the criticisms passed on the fair sex, several having nicknames from peculiarities or proceedings; one familiarly termed Miss Poult, which came to her from her using the term "a cruel poult" to one of our captains, into whose side her somewhat pointed elbow had been thrust as she and her partner were whirling around in a waltz. "Ah! Captain," she said, as the waltz was ended, and she thought it well to apologise for the blow, "I am afraid I gave you a cruel poult just now, but, upon my honour, it was my partner's fault, who led me round but awkwardly."

Pretty lips might have redeemed the uncouth expression "cruel poult;" but this quaint name for a blow in the side was long remembered and quoted.

I was on the move again soon, being ordered to join a portion of the regiment quartered in the outlandish town of Cappoquin; but how to get there was the difficulty, the only road being through the bogs and over a great mountain, famous for being the hiding-place of a band of robbers. To describe the Cappoquin of those days would be almost impossible. It consisted of one long street extending down to the River Blackwater, and continuing some distance along the river bank. There was one wretched inn, a good many whisky shops, a number of small hovels, tenanted by an extremely dirty crew of men, women, and children, with as many pigs as the inhabitants could afford to keep. These pigs, being the gentry paying the rent, had the best part of the cabins assigned for their use, and were much cared for, if not respected.

The children got round the fire, the dog and cat lay close to the pigs to obtain warmth, and the children, when sleepy, made use of the pigs as pillows. It was altogether horrible, and as savage as any scene in the darkest part of Africa. Sad, indeed, were all the family, and great the whillaloo set up by the youngsters when piggie was either sold or slaughtered to meet dire necessity; but on his place being supplied by another, the lamentations ceased.

This system of all pigging together, creating inconvenience and a disgusting smell, is worse than horrible. In wet weather the filth brought in was great—a result of there being only one exit from these cabins. The pigs came and went as they liked, indulging freely in the reeking manure heap placed for their convenience and delectation close to the door; and thus, filth and poisonous matter of all sorts found its way into the hovel. A disgrace to people, however poor they may be, is to be living thus, but a still greater disgrace to the authorities of the wretched town for allowing their habitations, highways, and byways to be thus polluted.

Strange as it may appear, yet the neighbourhood was unusually well supplied with country seats, the homes of dukes, lords, baronets, and wealthy gentlemen, whose ancestors had built castles and mansions hereabouts on the banks of the beautiful Blackwater. Could none of these try to alter this state of things? Would they have allowed the existence of such barbarity on any of their estates in England? Poor Ireland! Your faults are many, but all of them are not of your own creation.

Everyone in the neighbourhood showed us hospitality; dinners and balls being given to our honour at Lismore, and elsewhere; and as for shooting, fishing, and in the season hunting, we had as much of it as we wanted; but the accommodation in the barracks was very wretched, and these were badly situated and most inconvenient. The place certainly was detestable, and doubtless was the cause of many of our officers exchanging or retiring. One scion of nobility, afterwards a peer, and who hated Ireland, was in perfect despair at his surroundings, so he tried the inn, but not to gain by the change; the filth thereabouts being greater, too extreme even to be overcome. Neither tobacco smoking nor *eau de Cologne* could lessen the smell of pigs and whisky.

His future lordship was uncommonly namby-pamby, and certainly not made for roughing it, or to dwell at Cappoquin. He asked for and obtained leave of absence, but at the expiration of his leave, not being able to effect an exchange, and objecting, as he termed it, "to banishment," he eventually sold out, his place being taken by a rollicking Scotchman, whose spirits were unaffected by the surroundings. He was fond of practical jokes and reserved them generally for what he termed "the wild Irish."

Some resented these jokes, and wished to know who he was, and, indeed, who many of us were, giving ourselves airs, etc. etc. One fair dame of good blood was informed that I was an Irishman, the only one then with the regiment.

"I never heard the name in Ireland," said she.

"Of Dormston Castle? Of course, in Meath, as you say. Now I think I do remember it. An old family I should say," was now her reply.

So much for an old castle. Mrs. F. was like a goodly number of her sex thereabouts, who only valued a man for his descent; forgetting or probably being unaware of the witty remark made on the subject by one of her countrymen, to whom some man boasting about his ancestors. "Sure, then," said Pat, "you are no better than an old potato, for the best part of you is underground."

Perhaps Mrs. F. thought I was the son of some poor man, as being only an assistant surgeon, and with no private means, and if so, she was not far from right. The word "castle" sounded well, and the rest followed, as if castles in Ireland were not as common, or nearly so, as other dwelling-houses. Afterwards we became great friends. She did happen to know some of my relatives, and on her husband, the major, being taken seriously ill, she insisted on my being asked to attend. This I did, and as I would not accept any fees, I stood yet higher in her estimation. (I suppose this was a sign of good birth, but ill-natured folk put my proceedings down to affection for her charming daughter. Disinterested friendship was not believed in.)

Between the hospitality of Major and Mrs. F., and the invitations to dinner (often two in the week) from two old bachelor brothers, I managed to pass my time very pleasantly in this outlandish district. As to professional work at the barracks there was little of that: the troops were very healthy; but, strange to say, I had quite a large practice among the gentry in the neighbourhood, much of it owing to my being frequently called in by the village apothecary, who, distrusting himself, was always requiring "further advice."

It gave me something to do, besides adding to my income, as in *these instances* I took fees. I have mentioned the village apothecary, who, in his way, was quite a character. A little, short, squat, fat figure, a round Milesian face, beaming with rude health and benevolence, quick in language, full of wit and drollery, and ever ready to mount his cob or stump it at the call of sickness. He was in perpetual good humour, never turned up his nose at the work he was called upon to do—indeed, turning up his nose was almost an impossibility, that article in his features being of the order snub—but trotted off equally cheerfully, whether the call were by day or night, the caller rich or poor.

Having brought at least half the children of Cappoquin into the world, he was known to everyone, and doubtless was the receptacle of many strange and eventful histories. He had the field all to himself, and was passing rich on a miserable pittance of two hundred pounds a year at the utmost. To me in consultations he was always most deferential. It was almost ludicrous to see the venerable apothecary so obsequious to the young physician, and I wished he were less so. "Yes, doctor" and "No, doctor," became monotonous; but if I proposed anything new, then my little friend would certainly reply: "Sure, doctor, it's so. Bedad, that's the very thing to aize the poor body."

Then he would add in a whisper as I wrote out a prescription: "But sure, doctor, don't forget to order it to be made up in small doses." These were charged at eighteen pence each, hence the advantages gained by limiting the supply. Peace to his ashes. I think I can see him even now going down the street on his little cock-tail cob, with a shocking bad hat on his head, a big frieze coat, termed his upper Benjamin, dirty boots, with tops the colour of mahogany, one spur, covered with rust and mud, stirrups and bridle in keeping, and the horse as badly groomed as a tinker's donkey. I before said that the mountains about Cappoquin were the resort of robbers and scamps generally. Indeed, our soldiers were called upon pretty frequently to aid in catching these gentry; particularly when a murder was committed, a not uncommon event, as the people of the district held life remarkably cheap, and a week seldom passed over but one heard of a murder or an attempted murder being committed.

The scoundrels stuck at nothing, and I might have fallen a victim to their barbarity had not a clergyman and his pretty daughter preceded me by a short half hour over the mountain between Cappoquin and Lismore. I had been summoned over by the surgeon of the regiment to a consultation on one of our men who was taken alarmingly ill; and on arrival was informed that the reverend gentleman had been robbed and badly wounded two miles from Chlogheen and had been removed to the inn at the place.

After attending to the trooper, I was directed to proceed to this inn and give my services to the wounded man; but they were hardly required, for my reverend friend's injuries were somewhat imaginary. He had been more frightened than hurt, not even hit, but the daughter demanded all my attention. She too was frightened, but in a way not easily calmed down; indeed, it was some days before she got over the affair.

The peace which was to be so lasting suddenly became disturbed. Of course, everyone knew it would be so, guessing eggs when they saw the shells. The new king, with whom the French were so delighted, ceased to please, and one short year had driven away a love for peace, and re-established a desire for glory and perhaps revenge. The Battle of Toulouse, after all, did not fulfil the hopes of the allied nations. The Congress of Vienna had almost settled the affairs of Europe, when, lo and behold! Buonaparte once more appeared in France and was received with open arms by the people and the army which he had led so often to victory! the chosen of Europe, the pet of the people.

Louis XVIII., considering discretion the better part of valour, disappeared from among his fickle countrymen, and once again the resources of the allies had to be drawn upon so as to destroy for ever this scourge of Europe; though why the French, if they preferred Napoleon to a Bourbon, should not be allowed to retain their choice I never could see. Napoleon was cold-blooded, selfish, and ambitious, but he had the glorification and love of France in his heart, and showed by his government and laws that he knew how to rule, and not improbably was often driven into a war by combinations made against him.

Napoleon was a heaven-born general, and knew it; he was, too, a far-seeing and resolute ruler, very much the sort required to govern the French people; and had he been left alone might have acted otherwise than he did. Anyhow, he could have and would have licked all Europe, had not we Britons come to their aid; and with our money and obstinate resolve finally disposed of this clever but somewhat unscrupulous ruler.

It was not long before all Europe was in a blaze, and preparations for war on the largest scale were made everywhere; but the notice given was all too short. Napoleon had outwitted the whole of us, and, so far as one could judge, it looked very like his being once again the Dictator of Europe.

The call to arms was universal, and well responded to; but to judge by what was written in the papers and by general conversation, there was little enthusiasm. None cared to begin war again, or have increased taxation for the relief of a nation or nations proving themselves somewhat unthankful for former assistance. As for the hurried departure of Louis XVIII., that was rather an advantage than otherwise. He was a mere puppet; learned nothing by the past, being unable to see that things had changed and were changing.

However, all felt that war was inevitable, and that this disturber of Europe must be crushed; for so long as he was free or lived, thus long would there be war. It was necessary therefore to put him down, and with him destroy the power of the French nation to do harm and create revolutions; and to do this effectually a combination of the Powers of Europe was arranged, and their armies marched forth to meet those of Buonaparte.

It was not long before we received orders to prepare for active service. Two troops were added to the regiment, and almost before we could get things necessary for a campaign, the summons came for the regiment to march to Cork, making that our headquarters until we should embark for Ostend. We were under the command of Colonel Dalrymple and Major Griffith, officers who had distinguished themselves at Vittoria, Tarbes and Toulouse, and had for commanders of troops, officers second to none in the service. Few of these were young men; their promotion had been slow and supersession great, but their experience was large, and more than once in despatches had the names of Brevet-Major Thackwell, Captains Hancox, Whiteford and others appeared.

Benevente, Cacabellos, Corunna, Almendra, Vittoria, Orthes, and

Toulouse told of their skill and daring. Hopes ran high, and young subalterns talked gaily of promotion, of course anticipating the being killed as a thing; reserved for senior officers only. The feats of daring meant to be performed by these young gentlemen were numerous, and a little too much boasted about; the older hands knowing what real war meant, and the quality of the enemy they would have to meet, were more reticent; contenting themselves with swearing at Napoleon—swearing in those days was decidedly common—for not giving them sufficient time to make preparations.

Not very long after our arrival at Cork the transports were reported as ready, and after a pleasant sail down the river we embarked at Cove, going on board such ships as had been arranged previously for our reception. All know the result of this effort made by Napoleon to recover the throne of France. A short but very bloody campaign. How we met him at Quatre Bras, defeated him at Waterloo, and finally sending him as a prisoner for life to St. Helena; how Paris was occupied by the allies, and how French territory was protected, or rather how the nation at large was made to see how complete was their defeat, and were subject to the surveillance of foreign troops for two years, these being quartered upon them in various parts of the country.

I look back on these days with mixed feelings, and, looking, I often wonder what Europe has gained by such an expenditure of means and men! Have the French become less restless? Are they less capable of doing harm in Europe, and have they learnt anything of the value of peace and the necessity for law and order? I trow not. The Frenchman of today is very much like his predecessors, with an uncommon short memory as regards being defeated in battle and eating humble pie.

But I must return to things at home. The barrack was changed for shipboard, and as far as one could judge, a long and bloody war in prospect.

CHAPTER 8

Arrival at Ostend

I thought myself lucky when I found that the only companion, I was to have in my cabin was Mr. Carson, the surgeon of the regiment. He was a man of good parts, and endued with all those requisites which tend to make a sea voyage pass off pleasantly. To a lively disposition he added a fund of anecdote and great good humour, so I anticipated some relief through his society to the monotony of the voyage, which might be long or short, pleasant or horrible, according as the winds should decide. However, as he told me later on that he was a wretched sailor, and perfectly miserable at sea, my views of companionship were modified. Presently all the horses were embarked, and we hoped that the signal to make sail would be given; but the sailors told us the wind was contrary, and that, to judge by the atmosphere and appearances, we were not unlikely to be detained some time at our anchorage.

I took this as a hint that we might safely leave the ship for a while and save them a dinner by treating ourselves to the same at an hotel or inn on shore, but we determined to live on the provision made for us on board the ship by a grateful country; but the beefsteak was too tough even for my teeth, and putting our pride in the pocket, with appetites sharpened by the sea breeze, we gladly accepted a dinner sent to us by the mate of the ship, who, seeing our dilemma, in a rough sailor's manner, but nevertheless most cordially, offered us the remnants of a calf's head and shoulder of lamb. They were excellent to taste, but were served up in a manner not particularly clean or tidy; but sailors are no great sticklers for ceremony, and our appetites forbade us from being saucy.

The mate or master seemed to think that having obliged us thus far, he was at liberty to make use of our cabin for cooking purposes, and began to cook at our fire. To this we objected, and the result was he removed all his or the owner's furniture from the cabin, leaving us to manage as we best could with the scanty allowance allowed by the government to each officer on board a transport. It was a lesson to us to be civil to the man in authority.

Turning in later we found bed on board a ship not a delight. The mattress was of the hardest, and a high wind having arisen, the old tub began to roll about abominably. The next day showed no signs of improvement, there being no change of wind, so Carson and I discussed medical subjects and politics; these last leading to an argument for and against the return of Napoleon; my view being that if the French liked to have him as their ruler, they were justified in welcoming his return, and that a Frenchman's view of war and glory altogether differed from ours.

I think I had the best of the argument, and have never much varied in my opinions on the subject. One thing, Napoleon's return was a good thing for me; inasmuch as, the next economical proceeding to be performed by the government was a further reduction of the army, and I should have been relegated to half pay, and earning guineas by insinuating myself into the good graces of desponding old maids with chronic coughs and asthmas, and of crusty old bachelors, victims to living not wisely but too well.

Going on shore, I dined with friends, and took the opportunity of replenishing our larder, or rather of laying in some stores so as to make the rations more palatable. At the banker's I was agreeably surprised to find a sum of money had been placed at my disposal by my good uncle at Brighton, so I was relieved from any anxiety on that score, and returned to the ship in great spirits, as the wind had changed, and our starting at daybreak was a certainty; but we were doomed to disappointment. After unfurling sails and beating out to sea the wind again shifted, and after a large amount of general discomfort, and no little strong language from the sailors, we came about, and returned to our anchorage.

All this time we were utterly ignorant of anything that was occurring at home or abroad. Buonaparte might overrun Europe and we could do nothing until the wind changed. Of course, steam has overcome this difficulty in these days; but at the time of the Peninsular War and later on, the despatch of troops, either in relief or for war purposes, entirely depended upon favourable winds. However, next day the wind really did suit, and we cleared out of the harbour, and wonderfully beautiful was the scenery around.

One could not but admire, as we observed the deep but narrow entrance, and then its swelling into such proportions as would allow the British Navy to ride there in peace and safety. Thought was busy with me as we stretched out to sea. I could hardly divest myself of an idea that in this campaign against the French, things might be reversed, and Napoleon recover all and more than his former power. What, then, would become of Ireland? Would she be lost to England? Not unlikely; for the Conqueror would find the majority of my countrymen quite willing to receive him; but Ireland could not govern herself: she could not exist as a separate nation; but, attached to France, with such magnificent harbours as Cork, Dublin, etc. etc., it would be a bad lookout for Great Britain.

I was rather uncomfortable during the night, but it did not interfere with my appetite for breakfast next morning. However, it was very different with my companion: he suffered abominably, and was callous to passing events, even to exhibiting pleasure when we were assured that not improbably tomorrow night might see us at our destination, Ostend. It seemed our ship was a fast sailer, and we had to reduce our speed; the director of transports wisely ordering all the ships to keep together, as French brigs were on the lookout for stragglers, and, instead of Ostend, a French prison would end the voyage. It was a disappointment; for, instead of Ostend at nightfall, we had not reached the Isle of Wight.

It was sad crawling. Another day at sea brought us under the cliffs of Dover, and next morning opposite to Dunkirque, near enough to make out all the buildings in the quaint old town. There a breeze sprung up, and by four o'clock in the afternoon we safely anchored in the harbour of Ostend. That is, we took from the 9th to the 19th May in sailing from Cork to Ostend.

We were ordered to disembark on the morrow, and as soon as ready to start for Bruges, a town about twelve miles distant. There was, therefore, but little time given for preparation; and, having gone on shore, done the town, finding nothing in it particularly inviting, I returned to the harbour and sought my ship, having a rare trouble to find it among the many in harbour. My companion, the surgeon of the regiment, had been directed to take up quarters in the town, the better to arrange official matters. The next morning, at 4 a.m., our horses were disembarked, and I went in search of the proper authorities who were to furnish me with a route and instructions, the sick being made over to my charge; and with these I was directed to proceed by the canal in a barge to Ghent.

For the time we were attached to the 42nd Highlanders, who were also proceeding by canal to Ghent. This was pleasing news to me, having been quartered in Ireland with the 42nd, and being intimate with many of the officers. On reporting myself I was welcomed, and by none more warmly than by my old friend Colonel Campbell, commanding the regiment.

We started next morning, but there was little to interest one; a journey by barge on a canal is not a lively proceeding at best. The country round lay low, swampy, and intersected with canals, with here and there whitewashed cottages showing themselves on the cultivated places. I found the captain of the barge, or whatever might be his correct designation, an intelligent man; and, conversing with him, learned that as a rule the people of those parts were not anxious for Buonaparte's return, as it was sure to be injurious to trade and commerce; but that the present Government was contemptible in the extreme, and to such, even to be under Austria or England would be preferable.

It was very slow work travelling thus; but we seemed not to be in a hurry to catch Buonaparte, or else our allies were not sufficiently ready: however, we were quite in the dark as to passing events, and appeared to be waiting to see what would turn up. It was late at night before we reached Bruges, and after dining on shore we returned to the vessel, as we were to continue the voyage at three o'clock next morning. As the only cabin on board was occupied by the master, his wife, and family, we preferred a bivouac on deck to sharing these luxuries; and, wrapping ourselves in our cloaks, and tightly packed, we slept fairly well, troubling ourselves very little about cold or discomfort.

The next day's voyage was through a more interesting country; and, coming to a village and an inn, we stopped for luncheon, getting good wine and plenty of provisions at a moderate charge. Finding the deck of the boat somewhat confined, I did a good deal of walking along the bank of the canal, and for curiosity frequently talked to the cottagers and entered their cottages. These last were all clean and comfortable, and the peasantry happy and fairly well off. Their usual drink was coffee sweetened with sugar after a fashion not nice, though adapted for a people of an economical turn of mind. Sugar being an expensive article, was not put into the coffee as we do, but a lump of it was passed into the mouth and, having utilised it in sweetening their own beverage, they passed it round for family purposes. Coffee, tobacco, and gin seemed to be a Dutchman's idea of happiness, and possessing these he did not seem to care what else befell him.

At eight in the evening we arrived at Ghent, and I went ashore in search of a dinner and a more comfortable bed than that of the preceding night. I found both at a small inn near the canal, with a most voluble landlady, whose French was execrable, but who abused Buonaparte at a great rate.

Next day we disembarked, and I was quartered at Ghent long enough to know somewhat about the town and its inhabitants. The first was dull and uninteresting, but I liked the inhabitants, particularly the ladies, who spoke good French, dressed well, and as a rule were pretty. I object to the dog being employed to draw sledges loaded with market produce or men and women, the animal, with its make and soft foot, being ill adapted for draught work. Priests were numerous, but were not worshipped by the people as in Ireland, nor had they the same power over them. I am convinced that much of the misery to be found in Ireland arises from the ignorant teaching and bigotry of these priests.

Louis XVIII, was here, and went about in his carriage, accompanied by his brothers and a few followers; but none seemed to be affected by his presence, or troubled themselves about him. To me the people appeared to be wanting in modesty and respect. My landlady certainly possessed little of these articles. She entered my room as it suited her, without knocking—bedroom or sitting-room, it was all the same to her—and discussed freely on her numerous complaints without compunction. She insisted on my dining at noon, but I fought her, and would have none of it, though she was supported by pretty little Collette the maid, who was bringing in the paraphernalia for dinner. "*Oh, cela, est le temps de souper,*" chimed in Collette; but, after seeing my obstinacy, added, "*Mais c'est tout la même,*" and retired, leaving the wicked man to have his own way.

The regiment was quartered at Llydyring, about six miles away, so I frequently rode over to see my friends; though I could not but congratulate myself on being quartered at Ghent; but my joy was not of long duration, for soon after I was ordered to join headquarters, greatly to the grief of my landlady and pretty Collette. The change was for the worse. I was sent all over the place for a billet and expected to be satisfied with sharing a bed in a cottage with a smoking Dutchman, or, failing this, to sleep in the same room with an old man and his wife. Modesty forbad, and finally a room was found for me in the house of the *maire* of the village.

All this trouble to me might have been avoided had common care been shown by the authorities; for I learned soon after arrival that next day, at nine o'clock, we were to shift our quarters, and that the route was through Ghent, where I could have joined. We supposed that this march was the commencement of the campaign, but after all it was only for us to go into quarters at and about a village called Miscelbeck. Here there was not a single billet provided for us, so all was confusion, hunger, thirst, and bad language, and all this to be handy for a review under Wellington and Blücher.

Eventually, I got lodged in a very small farm house, having little to recommend it but the civility and hospitality of the owner. Forage not having been issued, I was glad to accept some hay and straw from him, and having seen my horses safely and comfortably provided for, I went in search of food for myself; but to make myself understood was a difficulty. My entertainers could only speak Dutch and I French or English, so we blundered amazingly; however, at last I got hold of some rashers and eggs, and these finished, asked to be shown to my bedroom, for I was tired after the twelve miles marching.

I was shown into the best room, and in it were five Belgic soldiers, all sleeping together on some straw, and my landlady evidently expected me to pig with them on the floor. Having no heart to turn them out, I went into another and smaller room, which was without a window, a sort of large cupboard smelling abominably; but there was a bedstead in it with some bedding, though this crib was only five feet long, not within my length by nearly a foot. However, I doubled myself up, and never slept better in my life.

As the review did not come off next day as we expected, I took the opportunity of strolling about the country and looking up some of my brother officers, finding that few of them were in better quarters than myself, but many in worse. All of us had one thing in common, the regaling effluvia of the dunghill under the bedroom window, as the Dutchman generally places his farm filth under his best room window. There was a tremendous growl at the dirt everywhere, and the want of accommodation.

Doubtless, all would have preferred fighting the French to hobnobbing two or three in a room, doing nothing. However, we were not consulted, and had to wait another day before getting the order to proceed onwards to a place called Sandelbeck near Grammont, where the review was to take place.

About noon next day the whole of the cavalry force in Belgium, between six and seven thousand men, with the artillery, were drawn up in three lines, and presently His Grace of Wellington, with Blücher, and very many more foreign officers on the staff commenced the inspection, being received with the usual salutes. The duke did not look well, but the old Prussian hero seemingly was so, and in excellent spirits. After inspecting the lines, the troops filed before them and performed a few manoeuvres. I was agreeably surprised to find our country being able to show such a fine body of cavalry, especially after the great reduction of establishment made on the proclamation of peace so short a time ago; and one felt assured that when the enemy were met all would justify the good opinion formed of them by the authorities on this day.

The review was not over until 5 p.m., and at its termination we were directed to return to our quarters at or about Miscelbeck, where we arrived late in the evening, decidedly tired and monstrous hungry. After this nothing was done. Some officers were shifted about into other quarters; indeed, we were scattered about all the small villages; and beyond occasional parades, there was nothing to break the monotony. We chafed at the delay, and could not understand the necessity for it. The inhabitants talked a *patois* of French and Dutch, indulged in pipes and gin; and we were not long in discovering that there was little if anything in common between us. Altogether, it was very miserable, and continuous rain confined us to our pig styes. Growling was the only thing to fall back upon.

On the morning of the 9th of June, we were turned out at 3 a.m. for the purpose of being inspected by General Grant, who ordered us to march to the old ground at Sandelbeck—a confounded bore to go so far for the purpose. He could easier have come to us, and inspected there; but march we did in the rain, arriving on the ground soon after seven o'clock, and then waited a long while for the inspection to commence.

As usual, General Grant found fault; but this did not depress us much, as it was well known that the gallant officer was somewhat innocent of cavalry movements; but Lord Uxbridge, who came on to the ground about ten o'clock, evidently thought otherwise, for he complimented the regiment in the most handsome terms, telling us we were as he had always known us to be, both willing and able to undertake anything; and that considering it was now four years since the regiment had had a field day, the movements were well and accurately performed. This was consoling after General Grant's abuse; the more especially as praise from Lord Uxbridge was not too common, and it was a universal opinion that his lordship was the first cavalry general in the British Army.

My friend Buckley insisted on my being his guest at dinner on our return to quarters; but we had to go in search of the dinner, which, after all, was only bacon and eggs. However, appetite and custom made us none too particular, and as we knew the state of affairs could not last much longer, we growled less and lived on hope, expecting every day to get the order to march into France; though the newspapers received from England said that we had so advanced, and evidently knew all about us and everything else. However, report said Napoleon had left Paris, and we anticipated some hard fighting before much longer.

It was wonderful with what indifference we spoke or rather joked with each other on coming events. To one, tall and big, the information was vouchsafed that his chances of being hit were good, so huge an individual forming a target not to be missed. To another, with an unusually prominent nasal organ, its liability to attract the enemy's attention to him was pointed out; and so on everlastingly. The jokes were more personal than polite, and fell hard on such as rode badly, or, rather, who were not thoroughly at home in the saddle.

CHAPTER 9

Sudden Orders to March towards Grammont

Little did we think whilst thus laughing, joking, and growling at the delay in advancing, that the enemy were close upon us; but it was so. Our information was bad in the extreme; at any rate, we were kept in the dark by the authorities as to what was going on elsewhere, and nothing ever came from the peasantry in the way of news. They knew nothing, and seemed to care less. However, the order to march came at last, and that very suddenly. On the 16th, about five o'clock in the morning, an order came directing us to march towards Grammont, coupled with the intelligence that the French were within eight miles of our headquarters. This last we disbelieved, supposing that had it been so, the information would surely have reached us somehow, or the people would have told us; but these were an apathetic lot, and took things as they found them.

They cared very little for our departure, indeed, appeared to be rather glad to get rid of us; but I believe this arose more from a desire to be relieved of the expense of keeping us than from a wish to see the French in occupation. We were off before seven o'clock, and after marching through a beautiful country, came to Grammont, but did not halt there for a moment, receiving orders to push on to Engien, where we rested for half an hour to give the horses a feed and ourselves the same, if the queer stuff served out to us could be rightly considered food. We were told that up to this day the town had been occupied by a regiment of the Guards, who had only that morning received a sudden order to march; so, putting all things together, we concluded that something unexpected had occurred—perhaps Napoleon had as usual outwitted the lot of us, and that a desperate action was pending.

Almost before the half hour had expired, allowed for our resting, we were again on the move, proceeding eight leagues further; but pushing along at easy pace was now out of the question. The enemy were not far away, as firing could be heard distinctly, and the road was crowded with artillery, infantry, and other cavalry, besides ourselves, all proceeding in the same direction, and, as far as I could judge, somewhat confusedly. There could be no longer any doubt that a battle was imminent, but where was left for surmise. However, no halting was allowed, and late in the afternoon we entered Braine le Carte; but tired and, in some cases, utterly wearied as were the troops, still the order was onwards; our way being through numerous villages and hamlets. The inhabitants of these seemed to be utterly callous, and gave us no welcome or help. They must have known that the long-expected war had begun, that fighting even now was going on in their midst, and that almost for a surety a terrible battle would come off in their neighbourhood; but their apathy and indifference was marked, and few seeing it could avoid disgust, and asking themselves whether such as these were worth the sacrifice about to be made on their behalf.

About 10 p.m. we reached the town of Nivelles, but pushed on through it for about two leagues, as the French Army was thereabouts, and had fought an action with us during the day, obtaining the best of it, though not an absolute victory. As we proceeded, we were met by numbers of men and officers, more or less seriously wounded, who were returning to Nivelles from the battlefield. They gave us to understand that they had been surprised, and to a certain extent defeated, but were masters of the field, and that the fight would be renewed at daybreak.

It was very late, midnight, before we reached our halting ground, and there we bivouacked, tired enough, horses and men, for we had marched from seven in the morning at least fifty miles. The place was called Quatre Bras, from the Nivelles and Charleroi roads crossing each other at right angles. We tried hard to sleep, our lodging being the cold ground, but after the long march and small allowance of food most of us were too much knocked up to get even a wink; besides, firing was going on to our right, and that disturbed us, for we knew not how soon we might have to repel our attack.

Before daybreak on the 17th, we were up and in the saddle, waiting for orders in no little anxiety, as the firing to our right had become louder and more continuous; but nothing came of it. The regiments stood on the ground where they had bivouacked, ready for action, and some rations were served. Seeing hour after hour pass away, and

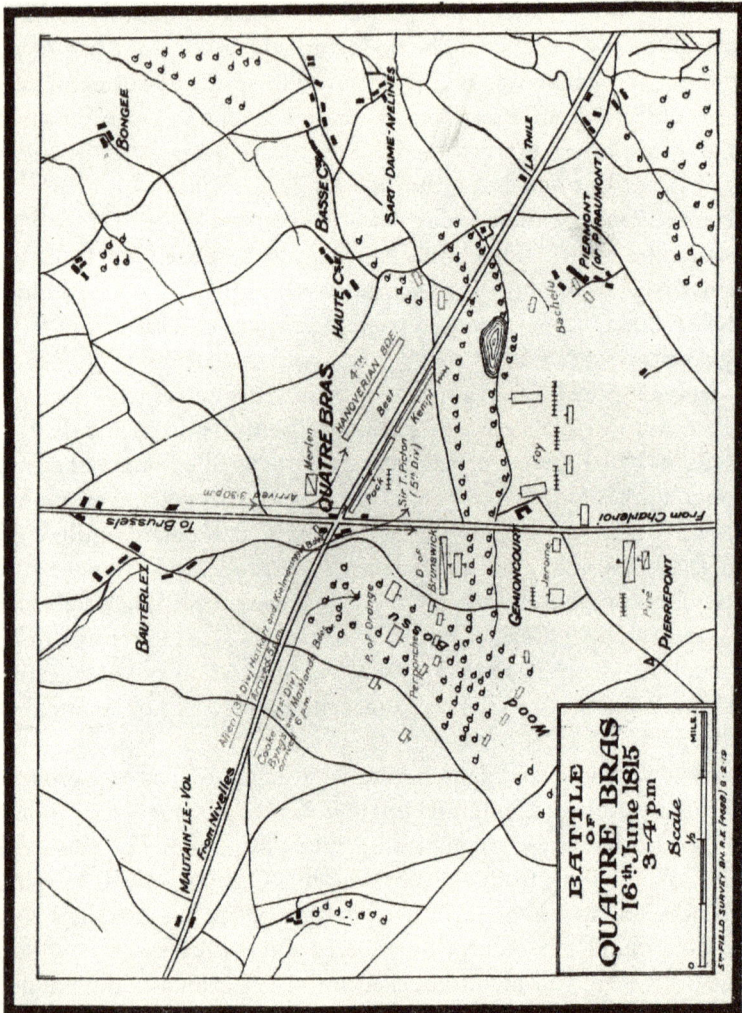

BATTLE
of
QUATRE BRAS
16th June 1815
3-4 p.m

Scale

BONGEE

BASSE CENSE

SART-DAME-AVELINES

HAUTE CENSE

LA TUILE

PIERMONT
(or PERAUMONT)

Bachelu

4TH
HANOVERIAN BDE

Best

Merlen

Arrived 3:30 p.m

QUATRE BRAS

Kempt

To Brussels

Pack

Sir T. Picton
(5th Div.)

roy

From Charleroi

BAUTERLET

D. of
Brunswick

Kielmansegge and
Allen (3rd Div.)

GEMIONCOURT

Jerome

PIERREPONT

R. of Ouatre

Perponcher

Cooke
Byng and Maitland
arrived 6 p.m

PIte

WOOD

MAUTAIN-LE-VAL

From Nivelles

MILE 1

½

0

BY FIELD SURVEY BY R.E. (1908) 6.2.13

Note :- Wellington took Command at 2-30 p.m. French Attack began at 2 p.m.

evidently neither party very willing to try their strength, I took the opportunity of riding over the field of battle, so far as circumstances would permit. It was a painful sight, and exhibited only too distinctly the horrors of war.

Dead men and horses, mixed up indiscriminately, were scattered about the field. Clotted blood in small pools, and corpses besmeared with blood, their countenances even now exhibiting in what agonies many had departed. Caps, *cuirasses*, swords, bayonets, were strewn everywhere. Houses, fields, roads, cut up and injured by artillery; drums, waggons, and parts of uniforms lying about; whilst every house or cottage near was full of wounded and dying; and this was only the commencement of the war. After all, we had no really hard fighting this day, excepting in the wood, though towards noon a brisk cannonade on both sides commenced, and continued until we were ordered to retire, as the French were too strong for us, and for other reasons best known to the Duke of Wellington; but report said it was for the purpose of getting into a better position for a battle on the morrow.

It was in a terrific storm of thunder and lightning that we retired, closely followed by the French. The retreat was across ploughed fields and corn, which impeding us considerably were of no assistance to the enemy. We continued to retire for about five miles, and when near Genappe, a regiment of French lancers attacked us, but they were repulsed in gallant style, notwithstanding being supported by artillery.

In the evening we took up a position near the villages of Mount St. Jean and Waterloo, but not without opposition from the French, who again attacked us, and managed to cut off some of our baggage waggons, which had separated from us. Later on, we sent out some skirmishers, who, after a little scrimmaging, returned, bringing with them several prisoners and horses. The prisoners seemed to be new hands and terribly alarmed, telling us that they had been forced to join Buonaparte. However, we did not believe them. A Frenchman never knows what he wants, is as fickle as the wind, and doubtless the whole French nation, supported by the army and navy, gave a hearty welcome to Napoleon on his return from Elba.

At dark the enemy's fire slackened, and then we fell back closer to the village and prepared to again bivouac; a wretched bivouac it was, far worse than on the previous night. Officers, men, and horses were completely done up with the long march of the day before and the continuous moving on this day, having very little to eat during the whole time. We were up to our knees in mud and stinking water, but not a drop of drinking water or a particle of food was to be found in the villages. We were half famished. We had marched and starved from our quarters in the village to Quatre Bras, and now had added a little fighting to starving and marching.

There was no choice; we had to settle down in the mud and filth as best we could, and those having any provisions about them were fortunate. As I had obtained a bit of tongue (but whether cooked, or only smoked and salted, I know not) in the morning, and had a thimbleful of brandy in my flask, I was better off than many, and finishing the somewhat queer tasting food, with others I looked about for a drier place to lie down on and rest weary limbs. It was all mud, but we got some straw and boughs of trees, and with these tried to lessen the mud and to make a rough shelter against the torrents of rain which fell all night; wrapping our cloaks round us, and huddling close together, we lay in the mud and wooed the drowsy god, and that with tolerable success. For, notwithstanding pouring rain, mud, and water, cold, and the proximity of the enemy, most of us managed to sleep. As for myself, I slept like a top, but I had become seasoned to the work, and was young and strong.

Very early on the morning of the 18th June we were ordered to bridle up and prepare for action. This we did in darkness, wet, and discomfort, but a night spent in pouring rain, sitting up to the hips in muddy water, with bits of straw hanging about him, does make a man feel and look queer on first rising. Indeed, it was almost ludicrous to observe the various countenances of us officers, as, smoking cigars and occasionally shivering, we stood round a watch fire giving out more smoke than heat. It was tedious work waiting for orders. We were anxious to be put into motion, if it were only to circulate our blood, for both horses and men were shaking with cold.

We had orders to form up on the edge of a rising ground near the farm of Hougomont, and there we remained for a long time unemployed; and seeing that this inaction was likely to continue, the interval was taken advantage of by food being distributed to both men and horses. At Hougomont, fortunately for our horses, some corn was obtainable and also drinking water. Oh! what a luxury this seemed to be, for not a drop had we had for twenty-four hours. However, it was not obtained without much difficulty, as the Guards, who occupied the farm, had orders not to admit anyone; and in their zeal, or whatever is the proper term for *punctilio* of that kind, refused us admittance, applying a rule for guidance equally to friends or enemies, single in-

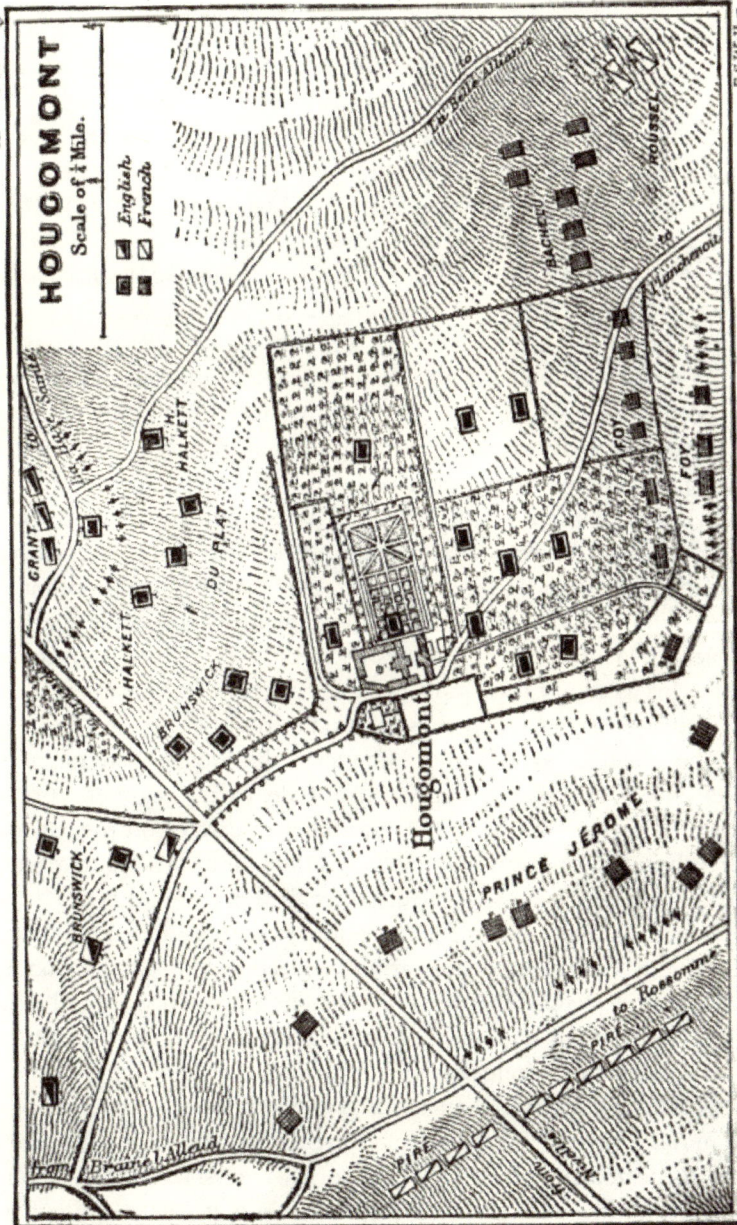

HOUGOMONT
Scale of ⅛ Mile.

English
French

dividuals, or, as in our case, a regiment of cavalry.

As to provisions, they were of the scantiest, and the meat was un-cooked, so it was not particularly useful, seeing that we had no means of cooking it; however, the men were not so particular as we were, for many of them picked the raw meat from the bones, excusing themselves on the score of necessity, and half believing that in such semi-cannibalism they made themselves fierce against the enemy, and would fight all the better; but, to judge by appearances, they did not seem to want this stimulus, for all were in high spirits and anxious for the battle to commence. (*Vide The March to Hougoumont: Lord Saltoun & the First Guards from Sicily, Walcheren and the Peninsular War to Waterloo, 1805-15* by John H. Lewis: Leonaur 2020.)

As the day became clearer and brighter, we saw that the country round was well chosen for a battle in which a vast number of soldiers on both sides must contend; the only obstacles apparently to men and guns being the very heavy state of the ground from so much rain, and the height of the standing corn. So high and heavy were the crops that a regiment of infantry could have been marched through it, without being distinctly perceived; but after these fields of corn had been marched over by three or four regiments it formed itself into a more or less solid mass, making a sort of cake over the swamps, giving a tolerable degree of resistance both to the feet of men and horses, which for us all just now was a great advantage, as guns, waggons, and the British Army generally moved into position.

About eleven o'clock of the forenoon, the French were observed as advancing, and that in a very gallant style, having regiments of *cui-rassiers* at intervals in the front, and bodies of cavalry on their flanks. For a short time, we did nothing, but as they came closer our artillery opened on them, and was immediately replied to by the enemy. The air was rent with the shouts and acclamations of soldiers, added to the ter-rific roar of the artillery of both armies. Indeed, so loud and continuous was this artillery duel, that you could hardly hear what was said by the person next you. It was evident that the battle had begun in earnest.

For some time, there was very hard fighting going on all round, every arm of the service being engaged. We appeared to fight so as to retain our position, and the French were equally determined to occu-py it. Repeated charges between the enemy's *cuirassiers* and our cavalry took place, in which we generally got the best of it. After a while there was a lull, each side appearing to be drawing breath, before renewing the struggle. It was almost solemn this pause, during which time I fancy many of us must have had some queer thoughts and sensations. As for myself, from the time the first shot was fired, during the heavy fighting going on in our midst, and up to this sudden lull, I own to feeling some indescribable emotion, not a particle of fear, very little excitement, willing and ready to join in the fighting, but withal a "*je ne sais quoi*," which I cannot explain.

But suddenly disgust took possession of me, my regiment was ordered to another part of the field, and I was forbidden to accompany them. I was to remain where I was. For the first time in my life, I hated my profession; my heart was with the old regiment. I had tasted a bit of fighting and rather liked it, and to remain alone, a mere spectator of passing events, was most unpalatable. If battle had had any terror in it for me, it had passed away and almost its novelty. I looked on at the struggle raging round me, more as a spectator at a field day than as one seriously interested in it. I believe that all my thoughts were concentrated in the fate of my own regiment; it was away in the thickest of the fight, and naturally I was anxious to know how all was faring.

I was not left long in doubt, as before a quarter of an hour had passed several wounded men had discovered my whereabouts, and after attending to their injuries I inquired concerning the regiment generally, but few knew much beyond what concerned themselves, they had had hard hand to hand fighting, but thought none of the officers had been killed or wounded. Whilst thus occupied an order came for us medical officers to shift our quarters, as there was no shelter for us whilst dressing the wounded; shot, shell, and bullets flying about in all directions. Indeed, we were exposed to the fire of the French artillery and their infantry, so were directed to take up our quarters in the village of Mount St. Jean.

It was neither an easy nor pleasant task to undertake, for the shot were flying about us in every direction, though in the sunken road we were somewhat protected. The huge cannon balls hissing and whistling over our heads, lodging with a terrible thud into the opposite bank, or striking the surface and rebounding, committed havoc and destruction in most unexpected quarters. Many of these missiles would have done comparatively little damage had the road not been paved, but on striking these stones the shot not only rebounded, but caused large fragments of rock to fly about, killing and wounding many who would otherwise have escaped.

I was through careless riding very nearly dismounted by one of these detestable cannonballs lodging in the bank just in front of my

15th Hussars charging at Waterloo

horse's nose. The animal stopped dead short, and instantly swerving round, brought me within an ace of a heavy fall. Serious as matters were, one could not help smiling or being amused at some things happening around. One of our *medicos*, who was not happy in the saddle, and whose seat on horseback was like to a pair of huge compasses, was cantering on in front of me, when first a shell burst over his head, and then a shot turned by some inequality on the surface, came bounding up the road, much in the manner pursued by porpoises at sea.

It was too much for the horse, who suddenly came to a halt, depositing the doctor on the broad of his back in the road; hard falling on stones and spent shot. On reaching the village we found our services at once put into requisition. It was full of wounded, and among them many of my own regiment, which report said had suffered heavily. We lost no time in doing our duty; but whilst thus occupied an order came from Colonel Dalrymple for us doctors to join the regiment, and so the surgeon and I again essayed the detestable paved highway.

The shot and shell flying about were if possible worse than before; but, thank the merciful Creator, we escaped, and proceeded onwards to where we expected to find the regiment, but it was not there, and no little difficulty attended our discovering its whereabouts, with fighting, cannon roaring, bullets whistling, and dense smoke all around.

At last, we got up to them, and were informed that the services of only one medical officer were required, and, being the junior, it fell to my lot to remain, Mr. Carson returning to Mount St. Jean. The regiment was halted and we were sheltered from all but shell firing by hugging the bank of a sunken road or lane, and here I received orders as to how I was to act when they engaged the enemy, and was informed of all that had occurred since we parted.

It was a terrible roll of killed and wounded; but the violent death of so many of their comrades did not seem in any way to affect the spirits of the men, who during this short interval talked most unconcernedly of the fate of their companions, describing the death of one man whose head had been taken clean off by a round shot, as if he had only lost a finger. The canteen of gin passed round from lip to lip as familiarly as if they were sitting in an alehouse, instead of on horseback waiting for an order to be again engaged. They were laughing and joking, made light of the weariness of themselves and horses, and declared they would yet be avenged for the loss of their comrades.

In the midst of this a staff officer rode up ordering the regiment to disperse a square of French infantry near at hand, and I was left alone in the lane to wait results. These were not long in showing themselves. The carnage must have been dreadful, if I were to judge by the number of wounded returning to where I remained, and that in a very short time.

As the day went on the roar of cannon appeared to increase, and any termination to the fight unlikely to occur. Both sides fought desperately, and were resolved to win; but as the regiment moved about, I was told to return to Mount St. Jean, where I could be more useful, and to which village most of the wounded made their way.

Nothing could exceed the misery exhibited on this road, which, being the highpave, or I might say the stone causeway leading to Brussels, was crowded to excess with our wounded and French prisoners, shot and shell meanwhile pouring into them. The hardest heart must have recoiled from this scene of horror; wounded men being re wounded, many of whom had received previously the most frightful injuries. Here a man with an arm suspended only by a single muscle, another with his head horribly mangled by a sabre cut, or one with half his face shot away, received fresh damage; but what made the scene more depressing was the knowledge that it was impossible to afford relief to all or even a goodly proportion of the sufferers, added to the conviction that for very many, their cases being utterly hopeless, time could not be spared on their behalf.

It was a cruel task to be obliged to tell a dying soldier who had served his king and country well on that day, that his case was hopeless, more especially when he was unable to realise the same for himself, and then to pass on to another, where skill might avail.

Some of the prisoners as they passed along the road to Brussels were communicative, not a few of them showing the duplicity of the French character or perhaps their love of change. As they passed many shouted *Vive le Roi*, and who but a short time previously were risking their lives for Napoleon; but honour be to whom honour is due: some there were who shouted for the emperor, and hoped that his cause might yet prosper.

About seven o'clock in the evening I was again ordered to rejoin the regiment, and doing so, it was with no little sorrow that I observed how terribly its numbers had diminished, and that many a dear friend of mine among the officers was killed or wounded. The contest seemed to me to be nothing diminished, but more general and desperate. The thunder of cannon and the rain of bullets were considerably augmented, men and horses every moment falling. To me,

WOUNDED AT MOUNT ST. JEAN

coming fresh on this part of the field, it seemed as if the French were getting the best of it slowly but surely, and I was not singular in this view, for a goodly number of experienced officers thought the same, and that the battle would terminate in the enemy's favour; notwithstanding our having driven the French from favourable positions, and holding our own against them.

Their numbers were overwhelming. The cavalry in proportion suffered more than the infantry, and now could move over the ground but very slowly, indeed often at only walking pace, fighting when called upon. During much of this time I accompanied the regiment, riding by the colonel's side, only quitting them or halting when they were charging squares, or opposing other cavalry. Again, I was directed to return to Mount St. Jean, and succeeded in arriving safely notwithstanding every difficulty and increasing horrors.

I had not been ten minutes in the village, indeed had hardly commenced giving my assistance, when the colonel of my regiment was brought in desperately wounded, he telling me it had occurred almost immediately after I had left his side. A round shot had shattered his leg, and entering the horse's abdomen, killed it on the spot. As the wounded limb was on the side near which I had been riding, it is not improbable that had I remained I also should have suffered. The leg was only suspended by a few muscles and the bone in splinters. Amputation, and that at once, was the only chance.

I got the colonel placed in a room where there were several other wounded officers, and separating the foot from its connections, told him he must undergo the operation of amputation. Then after obviating all danger from haemorrhage, I endeavoured to get him removed to a more suitable place for the operation; so, removing a door from an outhouse, we placed him upon it, and as we were leaving the dreadful room, I came across Mr. Carson, who suggested his being taken to Waterloo, there being more accommodation there. The misery to be seen in that room was more than dreadful, and I was anxious that Dalrymple should not be disheartened by it.

It was crowded to excess with wounded officers, many of whom were dying, and melancholy was it to hear their cries for relief, and to know that in only too many instances nothing could be done. There was not even a drop of water to be had so as to assuage their burning thirst, nor apparently any of the usual provision made for wounded men. Added to this, there was every probability of the village and our position there being assaulted by the enemy. The agony of some was

BATTLE of WATERLOO
June 18th, 1815.
7.45 p.m.

so terrible, that they prayed to be killed outright rather than endure excruciating torture.

With the aid of my door and six men we got the colonel to the village of Waterloo, about one mile distant, and sought for accommodation, but every house and cottage was crowded. Men and officers intermingled; many of whom as yet had not received surgical aid, and among these, to my great grief, I came across my dear young friend. Lieutenant Buckley of my regiment. He had received a bullet wound in the stomach, the missile had passed through his liver and come out through his back causing great haemorrhage. I hurriedly dressed the wound and gave him all the hopes possible, but did not conceal my misgivings.

It was a melancholy sight to find a youth of his age, perhaps nineteen or twenty, cut off in the very opening of life, and this his first battle. He had done his duty, and acted as bravely as the oldest soldier, and now dying, he behaved and spoke as became a Christian. I loved him well, but I had to leave him and rejoin the colonel, for whom as yet no place of comfort could be found. At length we were obliged to be satisfied with a miserable room and a more miserable bed or pallet in a small public house, where there was only one other wounded officer. It suited our purpose, and the people of the house were civil and obliging.

Towards nine o'clock the firing from both armies slackened, and soon after we had the satisfaction of knowing that the French Army was in full retreat, pursued by the Prussians, who had come up to our assistance late in the afternoon, having had some hard fighting beforehand. The British had fought Quatre Bras, and been more or less engaged next day, and it may be said, had been fighting or preparing to fight from daybreak on the 18th of June until darkness brought the awful struggle to an end.

Whether we should have won the day without the aid of the Prussians I know not; but of this much I am certain, that if the French had retired, we were too much exhausted to follow them up. However, we were not called upon for the impossible, and Wellington could not have left the pursuit in better hands than in the Prussians.

Few battles in history have been more hotly contested. The disparity of numbers and reliable soldiers was great, the French having the advantage in every way. The engagement showed skilful generalship on both sides, and brought out prominently the bulldog courage and obstinacy of the Briton. The result proved the invincibility of natural courage, a good cause, and an experienced general.

Transporting the wounded by La-Haye-Sainte to the field hospital

CHAPTER 10

The Horrors of War

Each side gloried in their general and each felt sure of victory. The French were said to have brought 74,000 men in the field, whereas our total was not 68,000, and of these many were badly trained Belgians. Let not this, however, detract from the bravery and skill of the enemy. They fought well, but were not fired with the same enthusiasm as ourselves, or was their cause a righteous one. The lust of conquest was Napoleon's one idea. In this conflict my regiment suffered considerably in officers and men. We had two officers killed, Major Griffiths and Lieutenant Buckley, with seven officers more or less severely wounded, Colonel Dalrymple, Brevet Major Thackwell, Captain Whiteford, Lieutenants W. Bryan, G. Bryan, Mansfield, and Dawkins, and of sergeants and men nearly half were killed or wounded.

The next day the regiment started in pursuit of the enemy, the senior surgeon accompanying it, whilst I was left in charge of the colonel and wounded officers and men hereabouts; the junior assistant surgeon being sent on to do duty at Brussels. The accommodation for the wounded in these villages was hideously bad: each house was packed to overflowing, every room was full as it could hold, and little relief given, often none. The cries of these wounded for help were heard in the street; but even this, bad as it was, was shelter.

In passing down the street next morning at daybreak I was horrified to see, lying about indiscriminately on each side of the road, wounded soldiers of every arm of the service in all stages of suffering; some imploring medical aid and others silent, only looking to death as an alleviation to their miseries. Of course, aid could not be given to all. The numbers lying about were too considerable for even a fair proportion to receive relief, and doubtless not a few perished from want of immediate attendance; though this last is applicable chiefly to the French prisoners, as our own countrymen naturally claimed first attention.

LIEUTENANT-GENERAL SIR JOSEPH THACKWELL WHO LOST HIS
ARM AT WATERLOO

Having promised Buckley to see him again, if possible, I went on to where he was sheltered, finding him still alive, but perfectly collected, though evidently dying fast. He asked for my candid opinion, and this I gave him faithfully, not attempting to conceal from him the impossibility of recovery. He told me he was prepared to die, and with the resignation of a little child breathed a prayer to God, and in a whisper, barely audible, said:

Write to my father. Say that in my last moments I never forgot friends, and that I die in peace, hoping that those I love will be satisfied with my conduct yesterday.

Then, as if recovering strength, he asked me about the events and termination of yesterday's battle, and was sensibly affected when he heard how gloriously it had ended for England. His brave heart even now seemed to rejoice in victory, and his enthusiasm and love of his profession hardly lessened in the presence of death. My duties demanded my proceeding elsewhere, but barely had I left him when kind death came to his release.

For three days I found full occupation. A field hospital had been established, and the wounded were better attended to. The colonel gave me some anxiety, though on the whole he progressed favourably. The patients now were chiefly French prisoners; the wounded on our side, so far as practicable, having been removed to Brussels. Many of these showed a great deal of heroism under operations performed on them, and not a few in their dying moments exhibited their love for Buonaparte by exclaiming, *Vive Napoleon*, and *Vive l'Empereur*, expressing themselves as happy in having been permitted to shed their blood and die in his service.

The village meanwhile became the seat of disorder; villagers and soldiers wrangling and disputing, and guns, waggons, and artillery tumbrils passing and repassing. Even now, at the end of three days, all the wounded had not been brought in, some of the French yet awaiting removal. There was a sad paucity of medical officers and assistants, but towards the last all was hurried, and none, I fancy, expected so prolonged and bloody a battle.

On the fifth day, as the colonel was doing well, I sanctioned his removal to Brussels, where the accommodation was better and necessaries obtainable. The colonel had a relative at Brussels, and his carriage being sent over for our accommodation, we quitted the scene of misery together. The road was rough and terribly monotonous, cut up by artillery, waggons, carts, and everything with wheels on which wounded men could be conveyed. Much of it lay in the forest of Soignies, which was in many parts yet thickly strewn with dead horses and dead soldiers, lying unburied. The sight and smell was anything but agreeable. Foraging caps, helmets covered with blood, mixed up with broken waggons, muskets, drums, and weapons of all sorts, showed how hard had been the fighting in this dreary forest.

Quarters were found for both the colonel and myself with a German family, and nothing could exceed the kindness and attention of the master and mistress of the house; but the inhabitants of Brussels vied with each other in caring for our wounded; houses were thrown open almost indiscriminately to all ranks if wounded. They were certainly well attended to, in many instances far too well, when the nature of their complaints was taken into consideration.

Besides Colonel Dalrymple and Major Thackwell, others of our wounded officers were now in Brussels; all these I visited as often as circumstances would permit, but my time was fully occupied, consequently accepting hospitality or seeing anything of Brussels was out of the question; however, my stay was short, for late on the 25th of June I received orders to join the main army without delay, and at once made preparations for departure. There were plenty of doctors in Brussels, both civil and military, but a great paucity of the profession with the main army advancing on Paris. The colonel was decidedly improving, and was affected at losing me. I too felt regret at parting, but my heart was with the old regiment.

Cracking a bottle of Burgundy with a wounded officer who had been a schoolfellow in Ireland, and consigning the colonel to the care of Mr. Jeyes, I started on the journey next day, having as a companion Assistant-Surgeon Moffit of the 7th Hussars, an old friend with whom I had been acquainted for some years. We resolved to push on without any unnecessary delay, and judging that the army in front of us would have pretty well cleared out everything eatable, we laid in a goodly store of provisions, consisting of brandy, gin, bread, beef, and sausages, a tolerable collection, rendering us, at a push, independent of a billet, at any rate, not obliged to satisfy appetite with anything found.

The whole was stowed away with the baggage on our spare horses, so that our appearance with the servants was rather ludicrous, reminding one of ancient knights and their squires, or to a certain extent of Don Quixote and Sancho Panza. My *compagnon de voyage* was of a most cheerful disposition, so the journey was pleasant enough. At

Hal, where one of our divisions was placed during the Battle of Waterloo, a gentleman, quite unknown to us, insisted on our accepting his hospitality to luncheon, and, nothing loth, we accepted, pushing on afterwards to Brain le Coute, where we obtained tolerable billets in an empty house, it having been vacated by its owners anticipating the horrors of war.

Indeed, it was wonderful as we passed along to see the number of houses deserted and left to the mercy of the soldiers. Many articles of value were of course lost, but some were hidden in the woods, and there, too, many of the proprietors were also concealed. But this was not altogether from fear of what might be done to them by the French, for, so far as I could gather, they both dreaded and hated the Prussians more, and the upshot of the campaign was yet uncertain.

It was no affair of ours, however: we saw our horses and servants made comfortable, and with a couple of bottles of good Bordeaux, supplied by the old maid left in charge of the house (a fixture probably), and our own provisions, made an excellent dinner, strolling out afterwards to see if there was anything young or pretty left in the town; but we found none; the beauties, with all the other domestic valuables, had been packed off, leaving nothing in the way of female remainders but such as were not likely to attract attention, their age and ugliness being a perfect antidote to gallantry.

Moffit was on hospitality bent, and, notwithstanding our having had dinner, must needs ask young FitzClarence to return with us to supper, and this sprig of royalty at once accepted, doing ample justice to our sausages and whatever was going, and for the early age of seventeen showed himself to be equally good at brandy and gin, but at smoking he was a failure; he tried very hard to appear as though he liked it, but nature refused to support him. The young man was of a friendly and confidential nature, and soon was as much at home as if he had known us all his life.

Throwing himself with the greatest nonchalance on my bed, which was in the room, he went into history, and with as much bad taste as want of feeling, he "supposed" he would have to go into mourning for "*the fellow* who was killed the other day at Quatre Bras," meaning the Duke of Brunswick, who fell gloriously fighting for his country. We were not sorry when he took his departure.

Passing through Mons, Sars, etc. etc, we entered France on the 28th, and at once were struck with the difference in wealth and prosperity existing among the peasantry of France and in the countries, we had passed through or been quartered in. Here many of the peasants' houses were not one degree above the miserable cabins in Ireland, and their persons equally dirty. There was a degree of indigence and desperation about them not observable among the same class anywhere else. The misery and privations suffered by this class was attributed to the effect of conscription, constant war making this fall heavily on the able bodied, depriving whole villages of their best men and leaving the fields to be tilled or cultivated by women and boys.

The wars of Napoleon caused the people to look upon glory as everything, and to become unsettled, turbulent, and indolent. Now in every town through which we passed the white flag was hoisted, but whether this show of loyalty arose from love for the king, who had bolted, or through fear of the Allies I cannot say. Certainly, during the short reign of Louis XVIII. the peasantry had a better time of it, and perhaps saw the value of peace, so may have been in favour of Louis, but almost to a man the army were for Napoleon.

Of course, there were some really for the king, and only too anxious to exhibit their loyalty, particularly if doing so cost them nothing; e.g., when the mayor of Forét billeted us on a surly farmer who was a known Buonapartist. For this sin, two officers, two soldiers, and five horses were directed to be entertained at his expense. It was miserably dirty and uncomfortable, and, as was to be expected, the friend of Buonaparte was no friend to us, proving a very disagreeable host.

Leaving early, we breakfasted at Château Cambresis, and then learnt that Louis XVIII. was at Cambray, only a few leagues away, being well received. Indeed, if loyal songs, white flags, placards on the walls, and *Vive le Roi* written on every post meant reality, then the king's return was a subject of universal joy, and his bolting unnecessary. Not to be cynical, one cannot help being surprised at his haste in departing, and perhaps wondering with our merry monarch on his return to England and observing the joy of the London citizens, how it was that they had done so long without him.

The means of communication between Paris and the rear were not good. Of really reliable news there was none, the authorities around being as ignorant of passing events as we were. Where the advancing army might be, or what had become of the defeated French, none seemed to know. Some said there had been another severe action, but which had gained the day deponent could not say; others asserted that Paris had been occupied without a blow; whilst a generally believed report declared that the Allies had sat down before the city and commenced a regular siege.

That we were following the track of the Allies was only too evident, for it was truly pitiable to observe how the country round had suffered by their march. Whole fields of corn destroyed by the passage through of cavalry, artillery, waggons, and troops of all sorts. The inhabitants were very few and seemed to be scared out of their lives. Their horses, carts, waggons, etc. etc., had been pressed into the service for the conveyance of baggage, sick, etc., etc., and in despair believed that they were lost to them, and that now for a long time to come all the miseries of war would be felt in their own country.

Many of the houses had been plundered, and wanton destruction pursued; but it was pleasant to hear that the owners attributed this conduct to the Prussians and Belgians, extolling the English for discipline and order. It may be so; at any rate I feel assured that no British soldier would have dared to plunder valuables, or attempt to carry them away with him. Death would have been the penalty for his folly.

Crossing the St. Quintin Canal, we made for Vermont, sleeping there, and after varied experiences of the French and their ways, owing to being quartered among different classes and in various abodes every night, I arrived at the headquarters of the cavalry. Sometimes in this journey my quarters were in a *château* with delightful old ladies (though even here the young and pretty were conspicuous by their absence), with whom I joined in duets or quartets, passing a pleasant evening, or perhaps the next night was quartered on peasants, who let me know that they hated us Britons cordially.

I found that my regiment was quartered at Temblay, a place with an upper and lower town, and a short distance further on, so I joined accordingly, bidding my friend and companion Moffit goodbye, and bringing our eight days' journey together to a conclusion. Certainly, as pleasant a time as ever I have spent. There was much to hear about; though, of course, as Moffit and I neared Paris we were not kept so entirely in the dark as to what was going on. We knew that Paris had surrendered to the Allies, and that Louis XVIII. was to enter it in a few days, and at the same time we were told that Buonaparte had followed the example of his predecessor and run for it.

The escape of the emperor somewhat took away from us the satisfaction derived from the occupation of Paris; but the inhabitants of the towns and villages also regretted the emperor's flight, and Paris yielding so readily. Among them Napoleon was preferred to the king, notwithstanding his love for war and contempt for human life.

CHAPTER 11

Paris

There was no little difficulty in my obtaining quarters. I came last, the place was small, and the Prussians had been there before us. At last, I was directed to share quarters with a brother officer, but in the house the only article of furniture left uninjured or not utterly destroyed was a bedstead, on which I spread my blankets, feeling infinitely obliged to these very destructive Prussians for even leaving me that. These gentlemen literally ransacked many houses, and we coming after them as we did, were uncommonly badly off. They were like a swarm of locusts, making all barren around them. Indeed, for miles round they seem to have wantonly destroyed all they could lay their hands on. If revenge for the French occupation of Berlin a short time previously was their object, they certainly obtained it.

It became rather monotonous day after day doing nothing, only so close as to overlook the city of Paris; but by way of passing time, accompanied by Moffit, I often strayed into the surrounding villages, as much from love for the country as to gratify curiosity in observing how much mischief a Prussian soldier could do. Farms, or even the most miserable cabins, had not escaped their inquisitiveness; all were empty, but Moffit managed to find hidden away in a barn an old hurdy-gurdy, and seizing the opportunity, he immediately exhibited his vivacity and talent.

Declaring the instrument only wanted a little tuning to be perfect, and contrary to my wishes remaining on the spot to perform this operation, he commenced to play in a most romantic, not to say ludicrous manner, not caring who saw him, or what they might think about him. Fancy an hussar with an immense pair of *moustachios*, a brilliant rig out of *cossacks*, with broad stripes down the same, a jacket over his shoulders, and a grand gold-laced foraging cap, sitting on an extremely dirty barrel in the middle of an old barn hugging a hurdy-gurdy and singing sentimental ditties!

A few days after this we received the order to move nearer to Paris, with the probability of our entering it; for as yet this had been forbidden, and were not sorry to find ourselves soon after daybreak *en route* for Cateau. The route lay to the north of the city, and crossing the high road from Noyette, leaving Gonnesse to our right, we passed very near St. Denis, obtaining a fine view of the heights of Montmartre, and some of the larger buildings; conspicuous among them being the dome of the Hospital of Invalids. We did a good bit of wandering, and had ample time to reconnoitre the country round. Indeed, we did not arrive until nearly midday, thanks to the good opinion of himself held by our major of brigade, who prided himself on his knowledge and colloquial capability as regarded the French language; unfortunately for us, he was lamentably deficient, but too proud to ask for the services of an interpreter, so we went much out of our way on the march to Cateau. (*Vide Guns at Le Cateau* by A. F. Becke & C. de Sausmarez; Leonaur 2013.)

Instead of saying "*Ou est le chemin a Cateau?*" his invariable way of putting it was "*Ou est le chimeney a Catty?*" so that the person interrogated having too much politeness to say he did not understand, pointed out the way to any town or village whose name bore the faintest resemblance to Catty. Part of the town was occupied by us, and the remainder by artillery, and the 7th Hussars, these extending towards St. Germain. We were comfortable enough, much more so than could have been expected in the crowded state of the place, and to our joy the restriction about visiting Paris was removed.

Malmaison, being within two miles, was first visited by us officers, and somewhat disappointed me. It was, as a whole, perhaps fine, but nothing superb, as some declare it to be. The picture galleries were good, and at that time untouched; that is, the spoil had not been distributed among the emperors and great men, but remained in the possession of Napoleon, or, rather, France. Report said that many of these pictures—"Herod Killing the Innocents," "Diana and her Nymphs Bathing," "The Holy Family," etc. etc.—were coveted by Alexander of Russia, and that he was bargaining for others. One wonders what became of the stolen pictures, and how was the restoration to the original owners carried out, if carried out at all. Some good mosaics, inlaid floors, and furniture were in the palace.

A day or two after this the regiment was inspected by the general officer commanding the cavalry; and then, to our disgust, a squadron was directed to change its quarters and march to Cariere St. Denis: this Cariere being a detestable hole, with only one good house in the village, in which all the officers attached to the squadron, myself included, had to be quartered. It was dignified by being termed a *château*. It belonged to a Monsieur St. Germain, who had fled to Paris, fearing the Prussians might do him bodily harm; but apparently, these gentry cared more for the contents of the *château* than to possess its owner, to judge by the way they had made love to everything in it, opening every press and cupboard, and not neglected the cellar.

However, there was enough for us, and we did not take advantage of the owner's absence and his vacant house beyond what our necessities demanded. The garden was well stocked with fruit and vegetables, and a pond furnished us with carp. After all, our change of quarters was not disagreeable. The view from the drawing-room windows, across the river to Malmaison and the surrounding country, was beautiful; so, we ceased to grumble, believing that a good house, a better garden, an absent master, and the cellar key in our pockets, were not to be despised.

It was not until the 13th of July that we obtained full leave to visit Paris; so, crossing the Seine, we soon found ourselves mixed up with the crowds pressing in the same direction. The grotesque appearance of the voitures, with their postilions, still more grotesque in their ways and dress, amused us greatly. These postilions were continually cracking their whips, and were dressed in a most eccentric if not absurd manner. A bright polished hat, with a cockade, was placed in most ineffable style on a mass of hair well powdered; this dreadful hair was extended behind into a very lengthy queue, profusely supplied with pomatum and powder, the whole tied up with a coloured ribbon.

The jacket, usually green or blue, was plentifully supplied with this powder, as it came off the queue, which bobbed up and down, keeping time with the trot of his horse, the rider not rising in his stirrups. The leather breeches fitted well, whilst the legs were lost in huge jack-boots rising high above the knee. These boots might have been made of iron, so stiff and unwieldy were they. Indeed, in some instances they were attached to the saddle, and the postilion had to jump into saddle and boots at one and the same time.

At about half a mile from the city an immense arch was building, eventually to form one of the entrances into Paris. In the Bois de Boulogne on each side the Prussians were encamped, not at all adding to the beautiful appearance of the city from this barrier. A little further on, we came to the square of Louis XV., only relieved from ugliness by the gardens of the Tuileries and House of Representatives; but I thought the view of Paris from this square grand and impressive. Napoleon evidently intended joining the Tuileries to the Palace of the Louvre, which report said would now be completed by the Bourbons.

Napoleon was bent on beautifying Paris, and all that he obtained through war and conquest which was rich and rare, he brought there. The triumphal arch in the square of the Tuileries was surmounted by a car drawn by four horses, of exquisite workmanship, stolen from Venice after the Italian campaign. However, it is not worthwhile to particularise all that was to be seen, and even now remains. Room after room in the Louvre was filled with stolen goods from all parts of the world.

The statuary was magnificent, and I lingered long there. "The Venus de Medici," "The Apollo Belvidere," "The Laocoon," "The Goddess Minerva," "Gladiator Dying," and figures representing the Nile and Tiber, and many others. In fact, I was bewildered in looking at acres of the works of the grandest masters the world has ever produced; but it was a pity they were not quite honestly come by.

If I were to describe all I saw and admired in this beautiful city, a three-volume novel would be a joke in brevity and dullness to my lucubrations; but there was something pitiable when one knew that it was a conquered city, and the conquerors were encamped in and round about it—a city of shame and should have been of sorrow, but of this little if any was visible. In the Palais Royal the gambler plied his trade without let or hindrance, and, when ruined, powder, lead, and a pistol could be found to blow out the brains, if he really possessed such articles. Women of the worst sort openly paraded themselves, passing off as daughters of Egypt, Spain, England, even Africa, and all to please the conqueror.

Gaiety seemed not to slacken; and a stranger, not knowing all that had occurred, would hardly have supposed that the people around him had been, not a month ago, at the mercy of a conqueror, their country occupied by victorious legions, and thousands of their relatives and friends either prisoners of war or lying dead, perhaps yet unburied, in the forest of Soignees or on the plains of Waterloo.

On the 24th July the Duke of Wellington's army was reviewed by himself and the allied sovereigns, so everything around us for some time previously was bustle and preparation. The space was too limited to allow of the whole force being drawn up in line, so we formed up along the broad road leading from Cateau to Paris, extending about four miles—a grand sight. The whole, after inspection, marched past the duke, receiving encomiums from the thousands of onlookers. The French made no secret of their admiration, openly declaring that the British cavalry and artillery were superb, especially the horses.

The review over, there were shouts and cheering. *Vive Alexandre! Vive le Duc de Wellington!* etc. etc., came from all sides. I doubt the sincerity of the majority. I expect that in their hearts they and the inhabitants of Paris generally wished us at the devil, only did not like to say so. The heavy cavalry brigade left soon after the review, and of course, we knew that our turn was coming; so, when the order arrived for our leaving the very comfortable quarters at St. Germain, the cellar, the carp, and the *château*, and to march towards Normandy, we were not surprised, but loth to leave. No more cellars well stocked with good claret, or gardens full of apricots, peaches, and vegetables, with the owner away for a holiday. However, I can honestly say that we respected his property, treating it as carefully as if it were our own, and never, from first to last, took advantage of the situation.

Our march was interrupted by a long halt at Fleures, where we found a hearty welcome from most of the inhabitants, and a very hospitable reception in the *château* of a M, D'Auteuil. Resuming the march, we arrived at our new quarters, Gisors, and were again in luck as regards billets. I was quartered on an elderly lady who over-enjoyed the good things of this life, and suffered accordingly; but, in her own opinion, she was amply repaid for the expense entailed in entertaining me, by receiving the benefit of my professional advice. Her Burgundy was excellent and her hospitality unbounded; moreover, her kindness procured me invitations from many of her relatives and friends, who, finding me musical and speaking their language correctly, made a great fuss with me, and insisted on my being their guest also. I endeavoured to make myself agreeable, and, being a great admirer of French ladies, let them see that I enjoyed their society. If only our women were endowed with the enchanting degree of animation so peculiar to the French, they would be the loveliest and most charming of their sex.

Our place was to be taken by the Prussians, and these being very much hated by the French, were unwelcome. Indeed, their advent was looked upon as a terrible misfortune. "*Oh, comme nous sommes fâchés; diable emporte les Prussiens; nous serons pillés par ces voleurs!*" However, there was no help for it, and amidst the good wishes of all, we started again on the march, arriving late at night at Rouen, not a little regretting the flesh pots of Fleures and Gisors. Halting here for a day, we proceeded to Trouville, where a lengthened stay was made, and where for the first time we heard that the treaty between France and the Allies had been signed, and that the British Army around Paris had already commenced to march homewards, but that our regiment was one of the many to remain in France, so as to ensure the terms of the treaty being carried out, and to keep the peace.

The treaty did not give our Gallic friends satisfaction. The terms were hard and extremely lowering to the pride of the French nation; but of course, it was necessary to tie them up tightly, and as far as possible to keep them quiet and free from war; but it did not seem to do so. Anyway, it perhaps kept Europe at peace, but as to Revolutions, changing kings and governments, that has been pretty constant.

Dieppe was our next move, where we remained for some time, not altogether to the delight of its inhabitants, who showed us scant courtesy or civility, and required being taken down somewhat, before they could learn that somehow or other, they must accommodate themselves to the new state of things. Many very disagreeable things were constantly occurring, although we honestly endeavoured to save their feelings as much as possible. This clemency, if I so may term it, was often mistaken for timidity, and taken advantage of.

One person, a well-to-do man enough, on whom was quartered one of our lieutenants, naturally a very quiet and good-tempered young fellow, found that he had made a mistake in his man. With an oath and a gesture of utter contempt for the British subaltern, he refused to acknowledge the billeting order, saying that the house which had been honoured by a Buonaparte should never shelter an English hussar.

"Ah! indeed!" replied the lieutenant; and immediately ordered the two best rooms in the house to be prepared for him, and with it accommodation for servants, etc. Finding that "needs must" when certain people drive, the rascal climbed down, and with inaudible strong language subsided into obedience.

In the middle of January, orders were received for the regiment to march to Auxy le Château in Picardy, and with no pleasing anticipations of our new quarters we started. Dieppe was dull and the people surly, but it had its advantages in being within easy communication of England; and report spoke badly of this *château*. However, it was time for us to be leaving Dieppe. Our men resented the treatment they received, and, losing patience and temper, commenced to let the inhabitants know and feel that they were a conquered nation; and this, though true, was to be avoided.

Through Eu and Abbeville, in due course we arrived at our new quarters, and found that the description of this Auxy le Château received at Dieppe, was true in every particular. We had to proceed two leagues beyond Château to a place called Bonniere and supposed by this, some advantage would be gained, but on arrival, to our utter disgust we were told that this Bonniere was to be our headquarters, and we to find billets in it. I was thunderstruck at the announcement, for of all abominable places, nothing could exceed the misery of this Bonniere. A wretched hamlet, consisting only of cabins, beggars, and mud.

On inquiry for my billet, I was shown to a hut, if anything worse than any Irish cabin. The inhabitants of it were not uncivil, but the place itself was a very dungeon, foul and disgusting. Asking for my bedroom or if they had such a thing as a bed, in reply they led me to a chamber without a window in it, the light being admitted through a hole in the mud wall, at present stopped up with an old hat to keep the bitter wind out. A mattress, or rather bedding of straw, no blankets, but a pair of sheets rough enough to excoriate the hide of a horse, with a bedstead not five feet long, and which could neither be removed nor added to, as it was jammed in between two mud walls. The floor of this delectable bedchamber was made of mud, the uneven parts of which formed themselves into small lakes, or deposits for water, not improbably for something worse.

For a moment I reflected on the difficulty I should have in discovering how best to recline on this bed, but I reserved this for supper as a consideration, and, being hungry, resolved not to go in search for the same, but to remain where I was. The town was too horrible in its roads and paths, now a foot deep in mud, to wander about, besides it was dark, and I saw no advantage to be gained by wading knee deep in slush at that late hour in search of a better billet.

Having some rations with me I had them cooked, that is I cooked them myself over the kitchen fire, broiling the meat whatever it was, and then sitting under the arch of the fireplace, which extended the full length of the room, with an old chair for a table and a three-legged stool for a seat, commenced my supper, when a man accompanied by a small boy entered the apartment, and, making a thousand bows and scrapes, bid me welcome, from which I gathered that he was the owner of the *château* near, being evidently better educated than his surroundings, as he spoke French grammatically and well, far better

101

than I had yet heard it spoken in Picardy.

After a while he informed me that he was the village schoolmaster; thus, accounting for his pomposity and language, that he received threepence a month for each *garçon* in his institution, and then must needs ask his eight year old brat to show off his parts for my edification, and thereby give me a good opinion of his system of polite education. He interrogated the lad as to the letters, vowels, consonants, etc., and between the two they made out a grammar unintelligible to me and particularly unwelcome to a man who was hungry, anxious to finish his supper or dinner, and more inclined to anathematise his beef for its toughness than listen to a village pedagogue.

Leaving my learned plebeian for bed, I hoped to sleep, doubling myself up somehow, but I was immediately attacked by something far worse than the poor schoolmaster or his enlightened son. These, with the shortness of the bedstead, spoiled my night's rest, and next day I lost no time in shifting my quarters. The new quarters I obtained were certainly an improvement on the last, and my hostesses were a couple of old maids, who were kind and tried to please me, lending me their pattens to keep me out of the mud and slush when I went my rounds; these, however, I so frequently lost or dropped, that I preferred wading and ultimately took to it.

This dreadful mud was everywhere: roads, paths, even fields, deep with it, and it necessitated all our officers using pattens, whenever they went out. Some exercise was necessary, and wading through the brook, which had a hard bottom, became a favourite walk, indeed was the only one. At the end of a week, to our great joy, orders came for our leaving this dog hole for Avesne le Conte. Pleased indeed were we to go, nor could I reciprocate the affection for me exhibited by one of my old maid hostesses, who absolutely cried at my departure, informing me with sobs that in their house never yet had there been a *gentilhomme*, "*avec tant de mérite*,"

The distance was short and did not remove us from the mud, nor was the change much of an improvement. I certainly preferred my withered old maids as hostesses to the new entertainer, a squat brandy seller of an affectionate nature, who invited me to share his dinner, placed his arm lovingly round my waist, and, horror of horrors, terribly nearly kissed me. Roughly and instantly, I pushed him off, giving him to understand that it was not the custom in my country for the male sex to embrace. Offended with his patronage and confounded familiarity, I refused his dinner invitation, and had the rations sent up to my room. He took the rebuff *à la mode Francaise.*

A short halt here, and we procceded to Bailleul in Flanders, and here we remained some time, being inspected by Colonel Doherty, who appeared to be satisfied with us, and who informed us that we were to make yet another move—rather disappointing intelligence, for we were heartily sick of this constant change of quarters. However, it was too true, and at the end of March we were again on our travels, the headquarters of the regiment to be stationed at Bourbourg and troops in Watten and adjacent villages.

At Watten I found a billet, an old woman hostess again, but kind-hearted, and we got along famously. Of course, it was rather dull, with nothing to read or to be done except visiting headquarters and watching the canal boats pass, as they did frequently between Dunkirque, St. Omer, Calais, Bourbourg etc. etc. The boats resembled those on the Grand and Royal canals in Ireland, but were much neater and adapted for passengers. They were frequently dragged by two horses, and that at a good rate of speed.

Rumour had been busy for some time with the report that our next move would be to Calaisso as to embark for England, and eventually it proved to be true. The order came, and we said farewell to the kind-hearted people at and around Bourbourg. For some reasons we were sorry to leave France, and the men felt making over their horses to the relieving regiment most acutely. Man, and horse had served together on many a hard-fought battlefield, had shared the bivouac, and they had marched together at home and abroad; so affection for the animal was natural. The inhabitants appeared really to appreciate the good conduct and discipline of the regiment whilst quartered on them, and entertained the men loyally the night previous to starting; that is *eau de vie* went round like water, and was only too willingly accepted. I fancy there must have been a good many headaches among the troopers when the order to march was given early next morning, and we started for Calais.

Perhaps my stay in France or my experience was not long enough to enable me fully to understand the French as individuals or a nation. They appeared to be contradictory in much that they did and said; abject in the extreme to their rulers whether kings, conquerors, or dictators, yet no people in any other part of the world could be found with such an unbounded share of self-consequence.

Every other name in comparison with *"le grand nation,"* was as a molehill to a mountain. One thing, this invincible vanity seared over many a wound and served a useful purpose under their then difficulties. Few, if any, of the sons of France allowed that they had been conquered, or that they were ever defeated in Spain or Portugal. The climate alone drove them out of Russia, and the whole army would have returned to France had not an old corporal blown up the bridge at Leipsic. They only retreated from Waterloo after beating the English because the emperor "was betrayed." I think the national character might be summed up in the word "restlessness," but they have very many redeeming qualities.

We were detained for some time at Calais waiting for the transports to arrive, and on their doing so we immediately embarked, and the wind being favourable set sail for England in May 1816. We assembled at Canterbury, and afterwards marched to Hounslow Heath, where we were reviewed by His Royal Highness the Commander-in-Chief. After a while, establishments were reduced, and, being placed on half-pay, I commenced private practice as a physician in the town of Cheltenham.

Historical Record of the Fifteenth, or the King's Regiment of Light Dragoons, Hussars

By Richard Cannon

In the summer of 1808, the regiment was removed into quarters in Essex, and was reviewed on the 19th of August by their Royal Highnesses the Prince of Wales and Duke of York, on which occasion the Duke of Cumberland commanded (as he always did when present), and their Royal Highnesses were pleased to commend highly the appearance, steadiness, and discipline of the corps.

Events had, in the meantime, taken place in the Peninsula, which occasioned the regiment to be called into active service, where the officers and soldiers gave proof that they possessed the military virtues of the field to an equal extent with those qualities for which they had been commended in quarters and at reviews. The attempts of Buonaparte to reduce, by treachery and violence, the Spanish and Portuguese nations to submission under his yoke, were followed by open resistance; British troops were sent to aid the patriots; and, in the summer of 1808, Portugal was delivered from the tyrannical rule of the invader.

A British force was directed to advance from Portugal under Lieut.-General Sir John Moore, to co-operate with the Spaniards, and towards the end of October eight troops of the Fifteenth Hussars, mustering seven hundred and fifty-three officers and soldiers, commanded by Lieut.-Colonel Colquhoun Grant, embarked at Portsmouth to join 1808 the army in Spain.

★★★★★★★★★★

List of the officers and number of soldiers of the Fifteenth Hussars, which proceeded to Spain in 1809:—

Lieut.-Colonel, Colquhoun Grant; Majors, Fras. Forester, Walter Nathaniel Leitch; Captains, John Broadhurst, E. J. McGregor Murray, Leighton C. Dalrymple, Edwin Griffith, John Joseph Seelinger, Hon. W. E. Cochrane, Joseph Thackwell, Alexander Gordon; Lieutenants, J. Buckley, John Whiteford, Skinner Hancox, Lewis During, Edward Knight, John Penrice, Charles Jones, Charles Carpenter; Cornets, Samuel Jenkins, James Laroche, Frederick Chas. Philips; Lieut. and Adjutant, Charles Jones; Paymaster, E. P. Henslow; Surgeon, W. Lidderdale; Assistant Surgeon, James Forbes; Veterinary Surgeon, James Castley; 7 quartermasters, 86 sergeants, 8 trumpeters, 674 rank and file, 682 horses.

Lieut.-Colonel Robert Ballard Long, and Captain Augustus Heyliger, on the Staff.

★★★★★★★★★★

During the voyage tempestuous weather occasioned the loss of twenty-two horses; and one transport, in which Cornet Jenkins, and twenty men and horses, were embarked, was captured by a French privateer. After plundering the vessel the privateer permitted it to proceed on the voyage, on condition that the soldiers should not serve until exchanged. The regiment landed at Corunna in the middle of November, and, advancing up the country, joined the division under Lieut.-General Sir David Baird, whose advanced-posts were in front of Astorga.

On entering Spain, Sir John Moore expected the co-operation of a numerous patriot force, but the small bodies of Spanish troops, which had been magnified on paper into powerful armies, had been broken, destroyed, or dispersed, and the small force he had with him was unable to cope with the three hundred thousand French soldiers in Spain. Notwithstanding this disparity of numbers, the British were ready to confront any danger, and to execute any enterprise which held out a chance of utility, and with the view of relieving the Spaniards at a critical moment, and of giving them time to organise their scattered means of defence, Sir John Moore ventured to advance against the enemy's communications, and to draw the whole disposable power of Napoleon upon himself.

The army set out on this enterprise early in December; the Seventh, Tenth, and Fifteenth Hussars forming a brigade under Brigadier-General Slade, with a brigade of artillery; the whole under Major-General Lord Paget, proceeded towards the Esla, followed by the infantry; they afterwards gained the right bank of the Douro, and continued their route in the direction of Valladolid. This direction of the march was, however, changed, with the view of attacking Marshal Soult's divisions on the Carrion; at the same time the British general, knowing he must eventually fall back, made preparations for a retreat. The Hussar brigade moved from Tordesillas to its left, a junction of the three divisions of the army was effected, and on the 20th of December, after a long and toilsome march, exposed to violent weather and snowstorms, the Hussars arrived at Monastero, Melgar, and Abaxo, in front of Mayorga, where the headquarters of the army were established.

Three leagues from the quarters of the Hussar brigade, between seven and eight hundred French Dragoons were in cantonments at Sahagun, under Brigadier-General Debelle; and although the Fifteenth Hussars did not arrive in quarters until late in the evening, they received notice, with great enthusiasm, that they were to advance 1808 and engage the enemy on the same night.

About two o'clock on the following morning (21st December) the Fifteenth, with Captain Thornhill and twelve soldiers of the Seventh Hussars, and Lord Paget at their head, moved along the left bank of the Cea, with the view of intercepting the retreat of the French Dragoons from Sahagun, while the Tenth Hussars, and four guns, advanced direct upon the town. The march was performed with difficulty; the weather was extremely cold, a deep snow lay on the ground, and the road was so covered with ice in many places that the men had to dismount and lead their horses. Between five and six o'clock the advance-guard of the Fifteenth fell in with a French patrol, and took five prisoners, but, owing to the extreme darkness, the remainder of the patrol escaped, and galloping back to Sahagun, gave the alarm to the officers and soldiers in their quarters; the surprise of the enemy was thus prevented.

The Fifteenth quickened their pace, and, approaching Sahagun a little before daylight, the French Dragoons were discovered, formed up, beyond a rugged hollow-way, which was unfavourable for cavalry, and, as the Fifteenth drew near, the enemy retired towards a bridge on their left. In numbers the French were about two to one, but British courage disregarding the inequality, Lord Paget moved the regiment, in column of divisions, at a brisk trot, parallel to the enemy's line of march, but some distance behind them. They endeavoured to cross the head of his column; when he changed direction. They then halted and formed for battle; as soon as the Fifteenth had passed the enemy's left flank, they were also halted and wheeled into line.

About seven hundred French horsemen stood opposed to between

107

three and four hundred British sabres; the disparity of numbers was great, but Lord Paget had unbounded confidence in his men, and he led the regiment at speed against the opposing squadrons. Stimulated by his noble example, the Fifteenth dashed forward with resistless impetuosity. The French, who had beheld the beautiful order of the march in column, had still the firmness to stand the charge; but they wore overthrown in an instant, and dispersed in every direction; pursued, and overtaken, some sharp fighting took place; many of the enemy fell beneath the sabres of the King's Hussars; two lieut.-colonels, eleven other officers, and one hundred and fifty-four private soldiers, were made prisoners; one hundred and twenty-five horses, several mules, and a quantity of baggage, fell also into the hands of the victors: the remainder of the French Dragoons escaped to Santarbas.

When this affair was over, Lord Paget expressed to the officers and soldiers his thanks for the very gallant manner in which they had conducted themselves; their superiority over the French Dragoons had been decidedly established; the loss of the Fifteenth was limited to two private soldiers and four horses killed; Lieut.-Colonel Grant, Adjutant Jones, eighteen rank and file, and ten horses wounded. The distinguished conduct of Lieut.-Colonel Grant was rewarded with a medal; Lord Paget also received a medal; the conduct of the Hussars was commended by Sir John Moore, and the regiment was subsequently honoured with the royal authority to bear on its appointments the word "Sahagun," to commemorate this spirited action.

From Sahagun, the Hussars advanced towards the Carrion River, and Sir John Moore made preparations for attacking Marshal Soult's forces; but he learnt that Buonaparte had put a powerful army in motion to crush the little band which dared thus to menace his line of operations, and therefore no time was to be lost in effecting a retrograde movement. The cavalry sent forward strong patrols, and preserved a bold front while the infantry withdrew; and on the 26th of December the whole were in full retreat towards the coast. The French legions hurried forward in pursuit, but were unable to gain any advantage of importance.

At Benevente, on the 29th of December, a body of Imperial Guards sustained a severe repulse from the picquets and the Tenth Hussars. A few orderly men of the Fifteenth were engaged on this occasion, and one of them was killed;—the regiment arrived at the scene of action; but the French did not cross the Esla a second time on that day; and the British resumed their retreat towards the coast.

During this retrograde movement, the services 1809 of the regiment were of a toilsome and trying character; exposure to frost, snow, and rain; want of provision, loss of rest, and the continual harassing duties of rear-guards, piquets, patrols, and occasional skirmishes with the enemy, put the bodily strength, constancy, and patience of the officers and soldiers to the severest test; yet, such was their conduct, that Sir John Moore stated in his public despatch:—

> Our cavalry is very superior in quality to any the French have, and the right spirit has been infused into them by the example and instruction of their two leaders, Lord Paget and Brigadier-General Stewart.

In covering the retreat from Bembibre, on the 2nd of January, 1809, the Fifteenth had three horses killed, and a few men and horses wounded, in a skirmish with the enemy; the regiment was also engaged in front of Cacabellos, on the morning of the 3rd of January, and again in the evening of the same day, when the British retired fighting through the town: the French Dragoons closed on the skirmishers of the Fifteenth twice, and had several men killed, but they did not succeed in taking a single man of the regiment prisoner. The French general, Colbert, was killed, and his squadrons were eventually repulsed. The regiment had four horses killed.

A squadron of eighty rank and file, mounted on the freshest horses, continued in the rear with the Infantry, and was repeatedly engaged while the regiment ascended the Monte del Cebrero, and traversed a country so broken and intersected as to prevent cavalry acting. The British Army was concentrated at Lugo, and offered battle, but Marshal Soult declined; and on the evening of the 8th of January the bivouac fires were kindled, and the army continued its retreat; the picquets of the Fifteenth Hussars remaining behind until the following morning.

Arriving at Corunna, the army took up a position to cover its embarkation, and on the 14th of January a picquet of the Fifteenth Hussars was on duty in front of the army. On the following day the enemy drove in the out-posts, and gained possession of the woody heights which overlooked the British position. Several horses of the piquet were wounded on this occasion, and a patrol under Captain Thackwell, who commanded the cavalry in advance, was sent by Sir John Moore to ascertain if the French were extending to their left. This patrol proceeded about five miles on the right front of the British Army without meeting the enemy, and part of the piquet of the Fifteenth remained on duty until the following day, but did not take part in the Battle of Corunna, where the British were triumphant, but where victory was bought dearly by Sir John Moore being mortally wounded.

The regiment had brought nearly four hundred horses from the interior to Corunna; the whole were destroyed for want of transport, excepting thirty-one, for which number conveyance was provided, and a few others, which were delivered over to the Commissariat. The army embarked and returned to England, and the Fifteenth Hussars landed at Portsmouth, Plymouth, and Falmouth towards the end of January.

This year the troop quartermasters were directed to be replaced, as vacancies occurred, with sergeants having the rank of troop sergeant-majors, and a regimental quartermaster was also appointed to the regiment.

In 1810, the regiment was stationed at Hounslow, &c., and was employed in the escort duty. On the 7th of April it was ordered to London to aid in suppressing the riotous assemblages of the populace which took place when the House of Commons ordered one of its Members (Sir Francis Burdett) to be taken into custody and lodged in the Tower. He was apprehended at his house, and conducted to the Tower by the Fifteenth, and a detachment of Life Guards; tranquillity having afterwards been restored, the regiment returned to its quarters.

On the 11th of June the regiment was reviewed on Hounslow-heath by His Royal Highness the Prince of Wales, who was pleased to express his approbation of its appearance.

Twenty thousand men were assembled on Wimbledon-common on the 10th of June, 1811, under the orders of the Duke of York, with the Duke of Cambridge second in command, and were reviewed by His Royal Highness the Prince Regent. The Fifteenth Hussars formed part of this force; and they were again reviewed on the 17th of June on Hounslow-heath, by the Prince Regent, in brigade with the Tenth and Eighteenth Hussars, and two troops of Artillery, under Major-General Lord Paget, who issued the following order after the review:—*viz.*

Lord Paget has the honour to announce to the troops of the Royal Horse Artillery, the Prince of Wales's Own, the King's, and the Eighteenth, regiments of Hussars, which he had the honour to command this morning, that he has received the commands of the Prince Regent to convey to them His Royal Highness's entire approbation of their appearance and performance. His Royal Highness was pleased to express himself, upon this occasion, in terms that were singularly flattering to every individual concerned, and to order that these, His Royal Highness's sentiments, might be made known.

During the following winter, and the summer of 1812, the regiment was employed in suppressing the outrageous proceedings of a number of persons who were combined for the purpose of destroying machinery in the manufacturing districts of Yorkshire, Lancashire, and Nottinghamshire, and who were called "Luddites."

The contest in the Peninsula had, in the meantime, been carried on with varied success, and during the winter, six troops of the Fifteenth Hussars were withdrawn from the north of England to proceed on foreign service. They embarked at Portsmouth in the middle of January, 1813, under the orders of Lieut.-Colonel Grant, and landed at Lisbon in the early part of February.

★★★★★★★★★★

Names of the officers of the Fifteenth Hussars, who embarked for Portugal, in January, 1813:—
Colonel Colquhoun Grant; Major Edwin Griffith; Captains Honourable W. E. Cochrane, Joseph Thackwell, Skinner Hancox, Philip Wodehouse, Thomas Dundas, William Booth; Lieutenants J. Buckley, Lewis During, John Carr, Edward Barrett, Ralph Mansfield, Isaac Sherwood, Honourable John Finch, Honourable Richard P. Arden, William Bellairs; Adjutant Charles Jones; Surgeon John Griffith; Assistant Surgeon Samuel Jeyes. Six troops of ninety men and horses each.

★★★★★★★★★★

After halting a short period at the capital of Portugal, the regiment commenced its march up the country, and was reviewed on the 18th of May, with the Tenth and Eighteenth Hussars, near Almeida, by Lord Wellington, who expressed his approbation of its appearance.

The Allied Army took the field with increased numbers and a superior organisation. The Fifteenth Hussars formed part of the force under Lieut.-General Sir Thomas Graham, which traversed the mountain districts of the rugged Tras-os-Montes, to turn the enemy's position on the Douro, and arrived on the Esla soon after the divisions under Lord Wellington had driven the French from Salamanca. At daybreak on the 31st of May, the Fifteenth Hussars approached the ford of Almendra, and entered the stream, with Light Infantry holding by the stirrups; at the same time the other troops approached the right bank. The stream was deep; the current rapid; several horses were pulled down by the infantry; others got into deep water, and many casualties occurred.

Captain Thackwell's squadron was in advance, and ascending the heights on the other side of the river, it was confronted by a piquet of the Sixteenth French Heavy Dragoons, who made a precipitate retreat, but were overtaken and some prisoners captured in Villa Perdrices. The French piquet continued its retreat, and was joined by other parties as it fell back; two divisions of Captain Thackwell's squadron pursued, and the 1813 other two remained in reserve, at the same time patrols were sent out on the flanks to prevent a surprise. For two miles the country was open; the French Dragoons occasionally halted, formed, and fired their carbines, but without effect, and this enabled the Fifteenth to come up with them, from time to time, to kill and wound several, and to make some prisoners.

Arriving at a fir-grove, the support halted; but two divisions of the squadron continued the pursuit until they approached an eminence beyond a rivulet, where nearly three hundred French horsemen were formed. The squadron of the Fifteenth being too weak in numbers to attack this force, it skirmished a short time behind the rivulet, and afterwards withdrew. The regiment had one horse killed, five rank and file and three horses wounded. One French lieutenant and thirty-five dragoons remained prisoners; a greater number were taken, but about twenty escaped, after having been left in the fir-grove.

The pontoons had, in the meantime, been laid down, and Sir Thomas Graham's divisions passed the Esla. The Hussar brigade under Colonel Grant advanced, and, on the 2nd of June, the Fifteenth supported the Tenth and Eighteenth Hussars, in the cavalry action at Morales, where Colonel Grant was wounded.

The Allied divisions were all in motion, and Joseph Buonaparte, being unable to stem the tide of war which now flowed against him, ordered his columns to fall back behind the Pisuerga River, designing to give battle there. The Allied Army continued to press forward, and the Tenth, Fifteenth, and Eighteenth Hussars were generally in front. As the army advanced, on the 12th of June, the French divisions under General Reille were found strongly posted behind the Hormaza stream, their right near Hormillas, and their left on the Arlanzan, thus barring the way to Burgos. The Light Division, preceded by the Hussars and a brigade of dragoons, turned the French right, while other troops attacked the range of heights from Hormillas to Estepar, and the enemy fell back in excellent order, passing the river by the bridge of Baniel.

The Fifteenth were on the extreme left, and advanced against three squadrons of French Hussars, who fell rapidly back for more than a mile, upon a body of infantry and some guns. Captain Dundas's troop, having been sent out to patrol along the left front, skirmished with one of the enemy's out-posts; but nothing of importance occurred.

During the night Burgos-Castle was blown up, and Joseph Buonaparte hurried his veteran army to the rear along the high road by Briviesca to Pancarbo, into which place he threw a garrison, and afterwards withdrew behind the Ebro. The British Commander instantly put his whole army in motion; the Hussar brigade passed the Ebro by the Puentes Arenas, and the Allied columns, urging their way through deep narrow valleys, intricate passes among rocks, and over lofty mountains, finally confronted the legions of Buonaparte in the valley of Vittoria. As the army advanced, some fighting occurred, and the Fifteenth Hussars supported the two British divisions which repulsed the attack of a superior force of the enemy at Osma, on the 18th of June. On the following day the regiment bivouacked in front of Sabijana Morillas; the French rear-guard was driven from the Bayas; but the ground did not admit of cavalry taking an important part in these actions.

The French formed in order of battle in front of Vittoria; on the morning of the 21st of June the Allied Army advanced in three corps, and the French were overpowered and driven from their ground with severe loss. The Fifteenth formed part of the centre column, which was led by Lord Wellington from Sabijana Morillas, by Olabarre, to the Zadora River, beyond which the French were in position. The enemy having left the bridge of Tres Puentes unguarded, Major-General Kempt's brigade passed at a running pace, and the Fifteenth galloped over the narrow bridge by single files. Some severe fighting afterwards took place, and Lord Wellington seeing the hill in front of Arinez nearly denuded of troops, moved a large body of men across the front of both armies towards that central point, and the Hussars followed in the same direction.

The Fifteenth supported the Infantry, and sustained some loss from the enemy's artillery; and, at length, the Hussar brigade, commanded by Colonel Grant, was ordered to advance on the left of Vittoria, to endeavour to cut off some infantry. The Fifteenth led the advance over ravines and other obstructions, and took some prisoners. On gaining a gentle ascent the right squadron formed, and was followed by the centre squadron; the left remaining in reserve; a regiment of French Dragoons advanced against the Fifteenth, who charged their opponents with distinguished bravery, and drove them back upon a column of about eight hundred Infantry, which was also broken, and laid down its arms. These prisoners were left in charge of the reserve squadron.

The French Dragoons rallied behind a body of Hussars and Lancers, and the two squadrons of the Fifteenth had scarcely time to recover their order, when they were charged by these troops; at the same time the Infantry resumed their arms, wounded several men of the regiment, and many of them escaped. The attack of the French Lancers and Hussars was met at a gallop, and the Fifteenth again overthrew their opponents; the enemy was driven in confusion towards the Pampeluna road, having many wounded, and others dispersed. The French Hussars and lancers had just been driven back, when a body of cavalry issued from the town and attacked the Fifteenth in the rear; it was charged by the reserve squadron, and by the right half squadron, which had changed front for that purpose, and this body of French also was driven upon the Pampeluna road.

During the confusion created by these attacks, the remainder of the prisoners taken by the regiment escaped. A squadron of the Tenth, and another of the Eighteenth Hussars, arrived to support the Fifteenth, but the French had reached the enclosures near the road, and darkness favoured their flight. They, however, left all their artillery, ammunition, and baggage, in possession of the Allied Army.

The behaviour of the officers and soldiers of the regiment under these trying circumstances was admirable; a private hussar took a French rallying colour, but thinking it of no consequence, he threw it away; another wounded and took prisoner, a cavalry officer who afterwards died at Vittoria. Colonel Grant, and Major Griffith, (who commanded the regiment) were rewarded with gold medals, and the honour of bearing the word "Vittoria" on its appointments was afterwards conferred, by royal authority, on the regiment. Its loss was ten men and four horses killed; Captain Hancox, Lieutenant Finch, one sergeant, forty-six rank and file, and sixteen horses, wounded. Captain Thackwell also received a contusion.

On the night after the battle the regiment bivouacked a short distance in front of Vittoria, and on the following day it moved in pursuit of the enemy in the direction of Pampeluna. In a few days afterwards it was despatched, with four divisions of infantry and two brigades of cavalry, to endeavour to intercept General Clausel, with fifteen thousand French troops, who had not been present at the Battle of Vittoria; but by forced marches he effected his escape through the pass of Jaca.

The regiment re-passed the River Arrogan on the 30th of June, and was afterwards stationed for three weeks at Olite, a town which was formerly the residence of the Kings of Navarre. While at this place the Tenth and Fifteenth Hussars were formed in brigade under Major-General Lord Edward Somerset; the Eighteenth were united in brigade with the first German Hussars, and Colonel Grant was placed at the head of the Thirteenth and Fourteenth Light Dragoons.

Marshal Soult having re-organised the French Army and obtained reinforcements, attacked the posts of the Allied army in the Pyrenean mountains, in the hope of being able to relieve the blockade of Pampeluna; the British Infantry fell back to a position in the mountains in front of the blockaded fortress, and the cavalry was concentrated in the rear of the line. The Fifteenth Hussars left their cantonments at daybreak on the morning of the 27th of July; they arrived at the foot of the Pyrenees, near Pampeluna, about five o'clock in the afternoon, and took post on the right of the troops commanded by Lieut.-General Sir Thomas Picton, whose left was at the village of Huarte, and his right extended to the village of Goraitz, covering more than a mile of ground. (*Vide Picton* by H. B. Robinson John William Cole; Leonaur 2015.)

On the following day the regiment was posted in the first line between two Infantry brigades of the Third Division, and on the 29th it covered the right of the position. The energetic efforts of the enemy on these days were repulsed by the firmness and valour of the British troops, and he was eventually driven back through the mountains to the confines of Spain.

After this brilliant success, the regiment remained for a short time in the villages near Pampeluna; it was subsequently removed to a greater distance for the convenience of forage, and in October, the right squadron under Captain Thackwell joined the blockading troops, where it remained until the surrender of the garrison at the end of that month. In October a remount joined from England.

In the beginning of November, the regiment advanced through the mountains to the banks of the Bidassoa, where it was stationed as a corps of reserve and support, during the attack of the enemy's fortified position on the river Nivelle, on the 10th of that month. Some difficulty being experienced in procuring forage, the regiment afterwards retired through the Pyrenees to the plains of Navarre;—it again advanced in the middle of December, and entering France, was cantoned at Cambo, and the villages on the right bank of the Nive, from whence detachments were sent forward to take the out-post duty in front of Urcuraye, to watch the valleys of Macaye and Mendionde, and the road to St. Jean Pied de Port.

While on this duty, the regiment experienced much difficulty in procuring forage, and parties sent out for that purpose had frequent skirmishes with the enemy's detachments; but the Fifteenth had not a single man captured by the French, although many narrow escapes occurred. On one occasion, Private William Darnell evinced singular address; he was at a farmhouse in front of the out-posts at Macaye, with men of other regiments, procuring forage, when a party of French Cavalry galloped down the road; he instantly ran to the gate, and fastened it in the best manner he could, which occasioned the French so much delay, that he had time to mount his horse, leap over some rails, and escape across the fields; the men of the other regiments, not being equally alert, were nearly all taken.

During the winter, when the forage in this part of the country was all consumed, the horses were fed on chopped furze pounded with a mallet, and, when it was practicable, they were led out to graze; they were also kept on a small ration of corn; but by the unremitted attention of the officers, and the exertions of the non-commissioned officers and soldiers, the horses kept their condition remarkably well.

In July, 1813, the establishment of the regiment was augmented to twelve troops.

Breaking up from their quarters in the middle of February, 1814, the British troops commenced operations against the enemy's left. The right squadron of the Fifteenth Hussars, under Captain Thackwell, pushed forward in advance, and had one man and two horses wounded in assisting to drive back the enemy's piquets. It was afterwards moved on in front of the Third Division; and, on the 17th of February, it established a piquet beyond the heights of Came, on the right bank of the Bedouze River, to favour the observations of the general commanding the cavalry, to preserve the communications between distant columns, and to watch the roads in that direction. It was joined on the Bedouze by the other squadrons of the regiment.

When the British general put his troops in motion to pass the

Gave d'Oleron, the Fifteenth formed part of the force which advanced against the bridge-head of Sauveterre as a diversion, to favour the passage of the main body of the army at Ville Nave. A small body of cavalry and infantry passed the river, but afterwards returned; the diversion was, however, complete; the French abandoned their works, and blew up the bridge, and the general operations were successful. On the following day the Hussars passed the river, and established posts towards the bridge of Bereux; and, on the 26th of February, they crossed the Gave de Pau below the broken bridge of Bereux, followed by the Third Division, when the French Cavalry posts were driven back, in which service the Fifteenth had one horse killed, three men and two horses wounded.

The Battle of Orthes was fought on the 27th of February. At daybreak, the Fifteenth Hussars, with the other regiments of their brigade and the Third Division, were formed in column of march on the Peyrehorade road, to cover the passage of the Gave by the Sixth and Light Divisions, and to protect them during their difficult advance up a narrow way between high rocks. During the engagement the regiment supported the infantry, and when the enemy's position was forced, it moved forward in pursuit. The conduct of Major-General Lord Edward Somerset's brigade on this occasion was commended in cavalry orders; and the commanding officer of the Fifteenth Hussars, Major Edwin Griffith, was rewarded with a gold medal. The regiment had one man and two horses killed; six men and five horses wounded.

Following the retreating enemy, the army passed the Adour River in the 1st of March. The Fifteenth Hussars formed the advance-guard of the centre column; they forded the river below St. Sever, and moved in the direction of Caceres. Arriving within a league of Grenade, the leading squadron, under Captain Thackwell, commenced skirmishing with the enemy's rear-guard, which defended for a short time the passage of a broken bridge over a rivulet. The right half squadron afterwards drove the French skirmishers through the town upon their support, and then charging the whole, forced above two hundred men of the Thirteenth Chasseurs à Cheval to fall back threequarters of a mile, upon two companies of infantry posted in the enclosures of a farmhouse near the road.

The left half squadron had halted in the market-place of Grenade, and the troop in advance, having detached so many men, that it consisted of only forty-five rank and file, under Captain Wodehouse, Lieutenant Mansfield, and Lieutenant Finch, withdrew from under the fire

117

of the French Infantry; it was followed by the *Chasseurs à Cheval*; but the rear division facing about, and galloping to meet its opponents, they fell back for more than a hundred yards. As the division of the Fifteenth again moved to the rear from under the fire of the French Infantry, the *chasseurs* took courage and advanced to charge, and were once more repulsed and driven back.

Thus, fifty British Hussars proved their superiority by boldly confronting, attacking, and forcing back more than two hundred French troopers; but at this period the British soldiers possessed a complete ascendency over the French, who, owing to a succession of defeats, had lost their confidence in their own prowess, and in the abilities of their commanders. The troop of the Fifteenth, having got out of the range of the enemy's musketry, made no further retrograde movement, and the French withdrew towards Caceres, leaving a number of killed and wounded, and about eighteen men prisoners. A greater number was captured, but during the affray several prisoners escaped across the hedges and ditches into the fields.

On the arrival of the head of the Sixth Division, the squadron of the Fifteenth advanced upon Caceres, exposed to such a heavy storm of wind and rain, that the men were permitted to put on their cloaks. Approaching a woody eminence, the advance-guard was stopped by a body of infantry and artillery posted among the trees, where private Robert Dalton had his cloak carried away from his back by a shell, which burst without doing any damage. The British guns coming up, the French were driven from the heights, where the out-posts were established for the night. On this occasion the regiment had one horse killed, six men and six horses wounded.

Lieut.-General Sir Stapleton Cotton expressed, in orders, his gratification at witnessing the gallant conduct of the officers and men of the Fifteenth, and recommended Captain Thackwell for the brevet rank of Major. Major-General Lord Edward Somerset also expressed, in orders, his perfect approbation of the conduct of the regiment; and added:

> With troops thus disciplined, the most complete success may be expected to attend the future operations against the enemy.

After gaining some further advantages over the enemy, the Allied Army remained stationary for a short time. On the 10th of March Lieut.-Colonel Leighton C. Dalrymple, accompanied by Captain Whiteford, joined and took the command of the regiment, and on the 15th Captains Philips and Carpenter, Lieutenants Douglas and Dixon, arrived with two troops from England.

The regiment was employed on the out-post duty, and furnished piquets at St. Mont and Carmillac. A hussar was posted on the tower at St. Mont, to watch the woods in the direction of the enemy, but a French patrol entered the place unobserved, and when he discovered the enemy, the difficult descent from his station rendered his escape doubtful; however, with great presence of mind and personal activity, he threw a bell-rope down the outside of the tower, descended by it, mounted his horse, and galloped away.

Marshal Soult made some offensive evolutions, which terminated without any important result. The British general being prepared for a forward movement, on the afternoon of the 16th of March the centre squadron of the regiment, under Captain Hancox, advanced in column of divisions along the road to St. Germier, supported by the right squadron under Captain Thackwell. The enemy's advance squadron was charged by the leading division of the Fifteenth with distinguished gallantry, and driven back upon its support, consisting of about three hundred men of the Thirteenth Chasseurs à Cheval. The centre squadron of the Fifteenth advanced upon this numerous body of opponents, who were driven back for two miles, to the village of La Cassade, when the pursuit was discontinued.

The right squadron then took the out-posts, and the French fell back upon Plaissance. Ten *chasseurs* were killed in this rencontre, an officer, thirty soldiers, and twenty-eight horses were taken; a greater number was, at one period, in the power of the Fifteenth, but many escaped, during the conflict, across the fields to the villages on the Adour River.

The regiment had one horse killed; six men and four horses wounded; one horse missing. Lieut.-General Sir Stapleton Cotton expressed in orders:

> ....his best thanks to Lieut.-Colonel Dalrymple. Captain Hancox, and the officers and men of that part of the Fifteenth Hussars which was engaged with the enemy, for their gallant and soldier-like conduct.

On the evening of the 17th of March, the English general pushed the Hussars up the valley of the Adour towards Plaissance, supporting them with the Light Division, followed by the Fourth Division; and at daylight on the 18th the whole army was in movement. On the 20th the French were driven from their position at Tarbes; the Fifteenth Hussars supported the infantry, and when the French fell back, the regiment pushed rapidly forward in pursuit of their right column; they, however, avoided the only ground where cavalry could act, which deprived the regiment of an opportunity of distinguishing itself.

The French Army continued its retreat upon Toulouse, followed by the British, and on the 25th of March the regiment was on the out-post duty in front of St. Lys, on the Touch River. On the 26th the squadron at Tournefeuille had to resist the attack of a body of French Infantry in a situation where it was unable to reach its assailants, and it had one sergeant, one private soldier, and eight horses killed; one officer, five rank and file, and one horse wounded; Captain Wodehouse had a horse killed under him, and another wounded. On the 27th of March the left squadron, after gaining possession of St Simon, found the place not tenable against infantry, and withdrew with the loss of one horse.

The town of St. Simon was eventually taken possession of, and the Fifteenth were stationed in it; they furnished the out-posts, but nothing of importance occurred; yet, to the credit of private James Wright, it must be mentioned, that, being on piquet, he attacked a French infantry soldier and made him prisoner, with his arms and ammunition complete.

In the early part of April, the army passed the Garonne River; the Fifteenth Hussars were in advance and took the out-posts at Gagnac, from whence patrols were sent out, and Corporal Winterfield and two hussars, being on this duty, fell in with a French patrol of the same numbers, who were made prisoners, with their horses. The enemy's piquets in front of Fenuillet were driven in on the 8th of April, when a corporal of the left squadron of the regiment was wounded.

At the Battle of Toulouse, on the 10th of April, the Fifteenth Hussars supported the infantry in their attacks upon the enemy's works, with the same intrepid bearing for which the regiment had been distinguished on former occasions; but no opportunity occurred for its engaging in close combat with the enemy; it was exposed, however, to a cannonade, and had four horses killed, seven men and three horses wounded. Its commanding officer, Lieut.-Colonel Dalrymple, was rewarded with a medal.

When the French evacuated Toulouse, the Fifteenth followed the retreating enemy; but soon afterwards the British saw their toils and conflicts terminated by the restoration of peace, and Louis XVIII. ascended the throne or France.

Thus ended a contest in which the mighty power of Buonaparte was overthrown, and the British troops had maintained their national character, and established their claim to rank with the first soldiers in Europe. The King's Hussars had been conspicuous, on every occasion, for their valour and conduct, and the regiment wus rewarded with the Royal Authority to bear the word "Peninsula" on its appointments, in commemoration of its services in Portugal, Spain, and France.

After reposing a few weeks in quarters, the regiment commenced its march on the 1st of June, for Boulogne, where it arrived in the middle of July, and embarked for England; having previously transferred thirteen horses to the French government for the guards of Louis XVIII.

The regiment was assembled at Hounslow on the 31st of July; on the 3rd of August it was reviewed on the heath by their Royal Highnesses the Prince Regent and the commander-in-chief, who expressed their high approbation of its appearance and movements. In a few days after the reviews, the establishment was reduced to eight troops, and in September the regiment embarked at Liverpool for Ireland.

While the Congress at Vienna was arranging the affairs of Europe, its proceedings were interrupted by the return of Buonaparte to France; the French Armies joined the invader—Louis XVIII. fled—and the resources of that powerful empire were once more at the disposal of this daring and ambitious chief. To dethrone Napoleon, and to give tranquillity to Europe, numerous armies took the field. Two troops were added to the establishment of the Fifteenth Hussars, and three squadrons, commanded by Lieut.-Colonel Dalrymple, embarked from Cork for Ostend, where they landed on the 19th of May; and, advancing a few stages up the country, were formed in brigade with the Seventh British Hussars and the Second German Hussars, under Major-General Colquhoun Grant.

★★★★★★★★★★

Names of the officers and number of non-commissioned officers and soldiers of the Fifteenth Hussars, which embarked for Flanders in May, 1816.

Lieut.-Colonel Leighton C. Dalrymple; Major Edwin Griffith; Captains, Joseph Thackwell, Skinner Hancox, John Whiteford, Philip Wodehouse, Fred. Charles Philipps, William Booth, John Carr;

Lieutenants, Edward Barrett, Ralph Mansfield, Isaac Sherwood, William Bellairs, Henry Lane, William Byam, Edward Byam, Geo. A. F. Dawkins, Henry Dixon, I. J. Douglas, William Stewart, John A. Pennington, Henry Buckley; Adjutant J. Griffith; Paymaster J. S. Cocksedge; Surgeon T. Cartan; Assistant-Surgeons, Samuel Jeyes and Wm. Gibney; Veterinary Surgeon C. Dalwig; 30 sergeants, 6 trumpeters, 390 rank and file.

★★★★★★★★★★

The whole of the British Cavalry, under Lieut.-General the Earl of Uxbridge, was reviewed by the Duke of Wellington and Prince Blücher, on the 29th of May.

As the regiment was reposing in quarters among the Flemish peasantry, it was suddenly ordered to advance, on the 16th of June, in consequence of Buonaparte having attacked the posts of the British and Prussian Armies. The regiment commenced its march soon after daybreak, arrived at Quatre Bras in the evening, and the allied Infantry having repulsed the French under Marshal Ney, it bivouacked in the fields, with a piquet on the right of the Nivelles road.

The defeat and retrograde movements of the Prussians occasioned the British to fall back towards Brussels. The Fifteenth Hussars were attached to the right column of British Cavalry, and their left squadron formed the rear guard in the retreat upon Waterloo. After passing the Nivelles road, some French squadrons intercepted a few waggons with wounded soldiers; and in protecting these, Captain Wodehouse's troop, with about an equal number of the Thirteenth Light Dragoons and German Hussars, charged the enemy, and took a few prisoners.

Arriving at the range of gentle heights in front of Waterloo, which was destined to be the theatre of one of the most important contests recorded in the history of the world, the regiment bivouacked in a rye-field exposed to torrents of rain.

On the morning of the memorable 18th of June, the regiment took its station in the first line, at the angle in the rear of Hougomont, from which the right squadron, and part of another troop, were detached to the right of the Nivelles road, and the Thirteenth Light Dragoons were added to the brigade.

While the battle raged along the line with incredible fury, the regiment suffered some loss from the fire of the enemy's artillery; and in the afternoon the brigade advanced to charge ten squadrons of lancers posted beyond the Nivelles road; but as the Fifteenth were moving to their right to cross a ravine, a large body of *cuirassiers* and other cavalry were seen carrying all before them on the open ground between Hougomont and La Haye Sainte, and their lancers were shouting in triumph. The brigade instantly moved towards its former post, and the Thirteenth and Fifteenth charged and drove back the *cuirassiers*, with the most distinguished gallantry, for some distance.

While pursuing its steel-clad adversaries, the regiment became exposed to superior numbers on both flanks, and was obliged to rally behind the line of infantry. From this period, until the French Army was overpowered and driven from the field, the regiment made various charges upon the enemy's infantry and cavalry of every description. At one moment it was cutting down musketeers; at the next it was engaged with lancers; and, when these were driven back, it encountered *cuirassiers*. Major Griffith was killed; Lieut.-Colonel Dalrymple and Captain Thackwell were wounded, and the command devolved on Captain Hancox. The officers and soldiers of the Fifteenth, like all their comrades in this memorable battle, evinced the most heroic bravery, and continued the fight until the French Army was driven from the field; about seven o'clock they halted; and the Prussians urged the further pursuit.

The regiment had Major Griffith, Lieutenant Sherwood, two sergeants, eighteen rank and file, and forty-two horses killed; Lieutenant Henry Buckley, and five rank and file, died of their wounds; Lieut.-Colonel Dalrymple—Brevet-Major Thackwell and Captain Whiteford,—Lieutenants William Byam, Edward Byam, Mansfield, Dawkins, three sergeants, forty rank and file, and fifty-two horses wounded. Lieut.-Colonel Dalrymple, Major Griffith, Captain Thackwell, Captain Booth, and Lieutenant Bellairs, had their horses killed under them.

In this battle the power of Buonaparte was destroyed, and the fate of Europe decided. The British troops received the thanks of Parliament; the expressions of the approbation of the Prince Regent; and the commendations of the Duke of Wellington. Their conduct was admired and applauded by the nations of Europe, and gratefully acknowledged by their own country. Every officer and man received a silver medal, and the privilege of reckoning two years' service for that day; and the word "Waterloo" was added to the honorary distinctions borne by the regiment. Lieut.-Colonel Dalrymple was further honoured with the dignity of Companion of the Bath; Captain Thackwell was promoted Major of the regiment, in succession to Major Griffith; and Captain Hancox was rewarded with the rank of Major in the army.

On the following day the regiment advanced in pursuit of the wreck of the French Army; and it was, soon afterwards, detached with other forces under Lieut.-General Sir Charles Colville, to invest Cambray, which place was taken on the 24th of June, and the citadel surrendered on the following day. While at Cambray, Captain Philipps of the Fifteenth was riding through some gardens, when suddenly the ground gave way under his horse's feet; as the horse was struggling, Captain Philipps threw himself from his back, and the next moment the horse fell to the bottom of a well eighty or a hundred feet deep, and was killed.

The regiment advanced to Paris, and when the capital of France had surrendered to the Allies, it went into quarters at Lion le Forêt, and other villages between Rouen and Gizors: in October it marched into quarters at Fauville, in Normandy, and afterwards proceeded to Dieppe, where it was joined by a reinforcement from England.

The regiment formed part of the Army of Occupation in France; but a reduction in the strength of the British contingent taking place, the Fifteenth Hussars were selected to return to England. After transferring two sergeants and twenty-five rank and file to the cavalry staff corps, and two hundred and fifty horses to other regiments, the Fifteenth embarked at Calais in May, 1816. The regiment was assembled at Canterbury, from whence it marched to Hounslow, and was reviewed on Hounslow-heath on the 1st of June, by His Royal Highness the Commander-in-Chief, who was pleased to express his approbation "of its appearance and discipline."

From Hounslow the regiment marched to Nottingham, Birmingham, and Wolverhampton, and in October it was employed in suppressing disturbances at Birmingham, on which occasion several rioters were wounded and others lodged in prison; Major Thackwell received a severe injury on the head from a stone.

This year the establishment was reduced to eight troops of sixty-two men and eight horses each; and, in 1817, an additional quantity of gold lace and embroidery was ordered to be worn on the officers' clothing and appointments.

In June, Major Thackwell was promoted to the rank of Lieut.-Colonel, in consequence of a former recommendation for special services in the field.

LEONAUR

ALSO FROM LEONAUR
AVAILABLE IN SOFTCOVER OR HARDCOVER WITH DUST JACKET

THE 9TH—THE KING'S (LIVERPOOL REGIMENT) IN THE GREAT WAR 1914 - 1918 *by Enos H. G. Roberts*—Mersey to mud—war and Liverpool men.

THE GAMBARDIER *by Mark Severn*—The experiences of a battery of Heavy artillery on the Western Front during the First World War.

FROM MESSINES TO THIRD YPRES *by Thomas Floyd*—A personal account of the First World War on the Western front by a 2/5th Lancashire Fusilier.

THE IRISH GUARDS IN THE GREAT WAR - VOLUME 1 *by Rudyard Kipling*—Edited and Compiled from Their Diaries and Papers—The First Battalion.

THE IRISH GUARDS IN THE GREAT WAR - VOLUME 1 *by Rudyard Kipling*—Edited and Compiled from Their Diaries and Papers—The Second Battalion.

ARMOURED CARS IN EDEN *by K. Roosevelt*—An American President's son serving in Rolls Royce armoured cars with the British in Mesopatamia & with the American Artillery in France during the First World War.

CHASSEUR OF 1914 *by Marcel Dupont*—Experiences of the twilight of the French Light Cavalry by a young officer during the early battles of the great war in Europe.

TROOP HORSE & TRENCH *by R.A. Lloyd*—The experiences of a British Life-guardsman of the household cavalry fighting on the western front during the First World War 1914-18.

THE EAST AFRICAN MOUNTED RIFLES *by C.J. Wilson*—Experiences of the campaign in the East African bush during the First World War.

THE LONG PATROL *by George Berrie*—A Novel of Light Horsemen from Gallipoli to the Palestine campaign of the First World War.

THE FIGHTING CAMELIERS *by Frank Reid*—The exploits of the Imperial Camel Corps in the desert and Palestine campaigns of the First World War.

STEEL CHARIOTS IN THE DESERT *by S. C. Rolls*—The first world war experiences of a Rolls Royce armoured car driver with the Duke of Westminster in Libya and in Arabia with T.E. Lawrence.

WITH THE IMPERIAL CAMEL CORPS IN THE GREAT WAR *by Geoffrey Inchbald*—The story of a serving officer with the British 2nd battalion against the Senussi and during the Palestine campaign.

www.ingramcontent.com/pod-product-compliance
Lightning Source LLC
Chambersburg PA
CBHW031858090426
42741CB00005B/546